Aldaniti

THE STORY OF A CHAMPION

Aldaniti

THE STORY OF A CHAMPION

Liz Tresilian

with pencil drawings by Caroline Binch

LONDON
VICTOR GOLLANCZ LTD
1984

Text © Liz Tresilian 1984
Pencil drawings © Caroline Binch 1984

British Library Cataloguing in Publication Data
Tresilian, Liz
  Aldaniti.
  1. Aldaniti (Racehorse)
  I. Title
  798.4'5   SF359.5.A4

ISBN 0-575-03482-3

Photoset by Rowland Phototypesetting
Bury St Edmunds, Suffolk,
and printed in Great Britain by
St Edmundsbury Press,
Bury St Edmunds, Suffolk

Contents

List of colour plates

7

Aldaniti

Jan Francis, Bob Champion, John Hurt and Jo
  Champion (Still by Bob Whitaker from the film
  Champions, a UBA production for Embassy Pictures
  released in the UK through Twentieth Century Fox)
John Hurt on Aldaniti (*Bob Whitaker*)
John Hurt on Aldaniti (*Bob Whitaker*)
Aldaniti with his owner, Nick Embiricos (*Ian Boyd*)
Aldaniti meets another National winner, Kilmore
  (*David Nicholls*)

Acknowledgements

I would like to thank all the people who have been so kind and helpful during the time that I was putting this book together. Nick and Valda Embiricos and their family were invaluable. Always ready to help—even over Christmas—their patience and assistance were incredible. Without them the book could not have been written.

Josh and Althea Gifford put up with both visits and a barrage of telephone calls, yet always found the time to help however busy they were. Without Mike Ashton's veterinary skills the ending to this story might have been very different: thank you too for having time to spare to help with Aldaniti's story. Tommy and Florrie Barron, and their son David, were also exceedingly kind, going right back to the early days for me, looking up records long put away, without which the story would have had no beginning. Thanks go, too, to Bob Champion for his version of many of the events. And to Charlotte and Jonathan Powell, who allowed me to spend hours pouring over Race Form Books in their house, as well as filling in a lot of exceedingly useful background information. Then there are Beryl and Wilf Millam, who must have come to dread the sound of the telephone ringing in the evenings as it inevitably meant yet more searching for dates through nearly ten years of diaries. Their patience and help was fantastic. Thanks must also go to my children, Crispin and Sophie, who did all the cooking and housework so that I could meet the deadline.

And of course Aldaniti himself—who stuffed himself with peppermints while he amiably provided a lot of interesting material . . . as well as extra personal detail.

CHAPTER ONE

The Ugly Duckling

The chestnut mare, her body heavy and pendulous with the foal she was carrying, was waiting in her usual place beside the gate when her owner, Tommy Barron, came to bring her in.

"Come along then, Polly my girl," he encouraged in the slow, quiet voice that the mare knew and trusted so well. That warm summer evening in 1970—seven foals after her arrival at the Harrowgate Stud near Darlington in Yorkshire, with the eighth well due—she would have followed Tommy Barron to her box like a dog. But on a small stud like Harrowgate, a thoroughbred mare in foal was too valuable to take risks with, so a halter was slipped over her head—a formality that they both understood.

Bringing Polly in was the last job before tea for Tommy —although from looking at her he reckoned that he and his wife Florrie were in for another late night. As the elderly chestnut mare waddled along the track beside Tommy, it was obvious to him that the long-awaited foal would be born that night. Turning her loose in the large white-washed stable with its deep bed of crisp, clean straw, Tommy patted Polly. "You might do us a favour and get it over early for once. Florrie and I could do with some sleep."

Polly's ears twitched in response as she nudged the man gently before turning away to the manger and the feed that she knew would be waiting. Although it was still light, and would be until late as it was June, Tommy switched on the stable light. He and Florrie knew from experience that mares hated to be startled or disturbed when they were foaling and the light had been left on each night in Polly's box for the past week so that by the time it was needed she would have become accustomed to it. Checking that the stable door was safely secured, Tommy turned towards the stone house that stood guard over the farm buildings.

"It'll be tonight," he told Florrie as he settled himself in the kitchen.

"Then I'll take the first shift," Florrie offered.

It was their way, when a foal was due, to work on a rota system, taking turns to keep an eye on the mare so that help was on hand should it be needed. They left the mares alone as much as possible, especially Polly, who turned funny very quickly when she had a foal. Florrie's offer to take the first shift was to cover the fact that even after years of breeding horses she still felt a sense of panic when she was the first to find that foaling had started. Polly had never once foaled at a convenient time—always well into the night, when it was too late to bother to go back to bed. So by volunteering for the first shift Florrie was fairly sure of avoiding the actual birth.

Florrie was still slightly in awe of Polly, the first thorough-bred they had ever had at Harrowgate Stud—although when she had first arrived it had looked as if she might well be the last. Shy, frightened, distrustful, the temperamental mare had been a handful for even the experienced Barrons to cope with. Bought by friends of theirs for two daughters to ride, the first time they had seen her she had been nothing but skin and bone: so bad that Tommy had said she would never survive. She had, though, gradually gaining weight. But as she became well again she proved too difficult for the girls to manage—a typical chestnut mare, awkward, contrary and sometimes downright dangerous.

The disappointed family had taken her off to a dealer and done a swop for another horse that appeared to suit their daughters better—until they had had it at home for a few days. That one, too, was a disaster. In desperation they had asked the Barrons for advice.

Living at Harrowgate Stud, not used any more, was the pony that had taught the Barrons' children to ride. Tommy and Florrie thought too much of the pony ever to sell it, or even let it live somewhere else. "Look," Tommy had suggested to his friends, "you get the thoroughbred mare back from the dealer—that Polly—and your girls can use our pony. It'll stay here, mind. Otherwise they can use it as their own—and we'll breed from the mare in return. There's good blood in her even if she isn't for riding."

Tommy's suggestion was easier said than done. The dealer sent many of his horses for meat. Polly, by then fat and well-covered, would fetch him a good price if he sent her for slaughter. He certainly did not want the other horse back as that had been difficult to sell—he had been glad to see the back of it, especially with a small profit. It was far too skinny to be worth sending for meat in Polly's place and too much trouble for him to want to have in his yard again. Persuasion and argument would not move the dealer. He was adamant that the deal had been done—Polly was going to the slaughterhouse the next time he took a load down.

In the end the Barrons' friends very firmly dumped the second horse in his yard. No more words were wasted. They walked out to the field, caught Polly up, and led her away, refusing to let the angry dealer interfere.

Harrowgate Stud was small, never more than half a dozen mares at a time. Tommy was trying to breed horses with a bit of size and scope that would go on and become National Hunt jumpers. Despite Polly's awkward temperament, Tommy felt that she was just the sort he needed to add a bit of speed to

13

the foals that he was getting, as well as bringing in the pure thoroughbred blood that they had not had before. Polly had arrived without any papers to prove that she had a pedigree, but after a lot of detective work the Barrons eventually tracked them down—and also the mare's real name, Renardeau.

To improve the standard of stallions standing at stud for a reasonable fee, and therefore the standard of the foals privately bred, the Hunters' Improvement Society had devised a premium scheme whereby good quality stallions that passed certain standards of pedigree, looks, performance, health and movement were placed in different parts of the country and made available to farmers and small breeders. Derek H was one of these Hunters' Improvement Society Stallions belonging to the Barrons who stood permanently at stud with them. Most of the mares he served were hunters with mixed blood of all sorts from shire to mountain and moorland. Pure thoroughbreds were usually sent to more expensive stallions. Polly was one of the few registered mares to come to him, and her foals by Derek H were the pick of the bunch on the Harrowgate Stud each year.

Standing at 16.2 hh, just a bit bigger than Renardeau, the dark brown Derek H added height and bone to the youngsters that the mare would have had by a smaller stallion. He had won twice on the flat and twice over hurdles before standing at stud. The reason that Renardeau—still known as Polly—was still waiting to foal that year as late as the end of June was that when she had first been put to Derek H in the summer of 1969 it was some weeks before the Barrons realised that she was not in fact in foal. Rather than have no foal out of the mare at all the following year they had put her to Derek H again, knowing that it would produce a late foal but that it would be worth waiting for.

Florrie went out for her first prowl round the yard just after dark. She waited quietly until the noise of a heavy lorry passing would drown any sound she made. Looking into the stable she saw Polly pulling at her hay—no sign that she was going to foal just yet. Relieved, Florrie crept away and back to the house.

"Nothing happening yet," she reported to her husband who was dozing in the kitchen. "It's strange to be out there on a warm night like this."

"Mmm." Sitting up for a foal to be born at that time of year was a new experience for both of them. Normally they had to do the work in the colder, unpredictable nights of late March and early April, as they had with the other two foals born on the stud earlier in 1970.

It was Tommy's turn outside when he heard the lumbering sound of the mare restlessly trying to bed down in a comfortable position. The foaling was quick. All over in a few minutes. As usual Polly had no problems, so apart from cutting the umbilical cord there was very little for Tommy to do. He watched silently over the door as the foal was licked and washed into life.

Just before dawn on 25th June 1970, the chestnut colt staggered awkwardly to his feet, fell over into the straw, scrambled up again, and wobbling dangerously with his legs spread out, took his first gawky step forward and found the security of his mother's milk.

"Well done my girl," Tommy said softly to the mare. "You did a good job there."

Later that day, when the sun was out and the colt had grown stronger, Tommy again visited the box. Polly's ears went back as she placed herself between her foal and the intruder. "Now then. Obsessive you may be, but it's time you went out." The familiar voice, quiet but firm, helped Polly to relax. She could be quite savage for the week or so after having a new foal, but she knew better than to take liberties with her owner. Keeping herself protectively between the foal and Tommy, she submitted to the halter being slipped over her head. "Just for an hour or two as it's such a nice day," the voice reassured her. "Your young fellow has got to see the outside sometime."

The colt was wary of this strange thing that led his mother

out into the yard. Determined to keep as close to Polly as possible, he almost fell as he walked out into the bright sunshine.

"I'll not put you with the others yet," Tommy told the mare as he led her to the small paddock near the house. "A few days on your own before you go back to your friends. I don't want anyone hurt."

Tommy was watching over the gate when Florrie came out to see the new arrival properly. Earlier she had peeped over the stable door, but all she had seen was a chestnut bundle asleep in the straw. Now all legs and head, the colt took a few awkward steps to explore as far as he dared, then staggered back to his grazing mother, nudging her with his nose.

"Right little ugly one," Florrie remarked. And that was the way he remained for the rest of that summer. Polly's colt was definitely ugly. There was no other word for it. He was going to be big, he had plenty of bone to promise height—but that was about all that could be said for him.

For the first time since the Barrons had bred from Polly, the mare was short of milk. There never seemed to be enough to satisfy the colt's perpetual appetite as he followed his mother round the field asking to feed, only to be nudged away time after time. Later, when Polly was turned out with the others and the chestnut colt played with the two older foals, he was raw and upright in comparison. Where they were well covered and round, he remained bony. Two months old, he was standing forlorn, hungry and dejected after yet another rejection by Polly, when the Barrons' son David, over from Northallerton, was watching the year's crop of foals with his parents.

"Chris thought of a name for him," he said to his mother. "She was just fiddling around. Now, you've got the four grand-children. If you take the first two letters from each of their names you get Aldaniti."

"Alastair, David, Nicola and Timothy. Aldaniti! I like that." Florrie nodded and looked at her husband.

"So do I," Tommy agreed.

At that stage the newly-named colt had had little contact with the humans around the farm. But they interested him, and he was already brave. Seeing a group of them standing there he trotted over to investigate.

"That's settled then. You've got a name at last," Florrie said. "None of that now," she added sternly as the foal took a pull at her dress to see what it tasted like.

The sharp voice surprised him. Aldaniti galloped back to the safety of his mother, head in the air, long legs stretching out. After a fright like that he needed both food and comfort. He pushed his head urgently underneath Polly. The mare did not want to know. With a sharp nudge of her nose she pushed him away and turned so that he could not get at her.

"It's no good leaving him like that," Tommy decided. "We'll wean him when we do the others. I was going to leave him longer seeing how late he was born, but she just hasn't got the milk to give him."

"She's getting older," Florrie pointed out. "But even still I've never known her do a foal so badly. A year without one will do her good."

The decision not to put Polly in foal again immediately had been taken so that they did not have another late foal the next year, and also because they all felt that she was getting too old to breed every year.

"He's raw compared to the others," David said. "He —don't get me wrong—just hasn't got the same zip the others have."

Aldaniti looked from his mother to the group by the fence as if he knew they were discussing him. But he was still hungry: that was the most important thing on his mind. Hopefully he took a mouthful of grass. Having got it, he did not know what to do with it and let it fall to the ground.

"Get him on to trough feeding with another foal. He'll soon pick up," Tommy said.

"Foals aren't foals for long," Florrie stated philosophically. "He's big. And he's strong. He may surprise us all one day."

Despite her near rejection of the foal, Polly was furious

when she found herself separated from him at weaning time in September. Shut firmly in her stable with the top door closed, she made sure that her indignation was heard by everyone. Nor was Aldaniti any happier, also alone, hungry and disconsolate. Out of his mother's hearing, unable to hear her complaints either, he had plenty to tell the world. For a few days Harrowgate Stud was not its usual peaceful self. Angry screams rang across the farm day and night, mainly from the foals. The mares had all been through it before. It was not long before they were being let out again and settling down to life, remembering the pleasures of having a foal beside them, but no longer fretting.

The foals were not so quick to adjust. To start with, none of them had been confined before. No familiar mare for comfort, on top of the move from open fields to being enclosed between four walls was bad enough—then there was the strange new food that was brought to them that they did not know what to do with. Aldaniti, at first still hoping for the milk that he had never had enough of, would push his nose deep into the trough, scattering the dry feed on to the floor, only to search the empty container unsuccessfully for what he considered proper food. Soon, though, desperation forced him to chew the strange offerings until he began to look forward to them and found that they did satisfy him, so that for the first time in his life he no longer felt hungry.

It was not long before he was being turned out with the other foals. Then, when the cold nights set in and he was brought in each evening of his first winter, the naturally friendly colt quickly lost all fear of humans. He learnt what a halter was for, and the basic manners that were to stay with him for life—the main point being that it was easier to do what Tommy wanted him to than receive a scolding or even a smack for showing that he had a mind of his own.

The three foals played in their field during the day between eating, drinking and sleeping. As the weather grew colder they were pleased to come in at night—Aldaniti, in particular, as he led the charge to the gate when he heard Tommy's voice

calling. By the following spring of 1971, when he was officially one year old, the colt had filled out. Although still growing
fast, taller at the back than the front, he already had that little
bit extra to him that made him stand out from the others.

"He really is in a class of his own," David said one day when
he was up at his parents' stud and the yearlings were cantering
about the field. "He's smashing."

Sensibly the Barrons let their youngsters winter out the
second time. A wise precaution in case it was ever expected of
them later in life, in which case they would have experienced it
early enough to be able to cope again. Aldaniti, now firm
favourite with the family, was left out with his friends. There
was plenty of shelter; hay and feeds were brought out every
day whatever the weather. Despite his thoroughbred blood,
the young chestnut enjoyed himself and did well, instinct
telling him that it was better not to stand around in the rain;
that cantering about with the other youngsters on frosty
mornings soon warmed him up, and in the new year that great
pleasure could be found rolling and digging in the snow.

By the spring of 1972, when his thick winter coat was
pushed out by the lighter, shining, summer coat, the Barrons
were even more pleased with the two-year-old Aldaniti.

They all felt that he was that bit more special—there was
something out of the ordinary about him, as well as his exceedingly kind temperament and gentle manner. So Aldaniti
was entered for the young hunter class at Northallerton
Show, to be judged by Tim Maloney. Shown in hand as he
was too young to be ridden, trotting out proudly beside
Tommy, he won easily. None of the Barrons were at all
surprised as he had fulfilled his potential in size, being big for
his age, despite his late birth. He had a lot of bone and, even at
that age, an air about him that caught the eye.

Proud of the rosette tied to his bridle, he accepted the
congratulations of his owners as calmly as his adaptable nature
had accepted the unfamiliar bustle and noises of the show-
ground. The journey home in the lorry did not bother him
either: he took it all in his stride and ate his evening meal as

quietly as if he had travelled and won every day of his life. After another winter out, growing, eating and developing all round, he had improved even more.

"He's none the worse for Polly not doing him so well," Tommy commented. "He's the most promising of the bunch. As he was foaled late we'll not hurry him. Give him until the autumn. Then we'll think of breaking him in."

David Barron, who held a permit for training hunter chasers, had his own yard at Northallerton. It was well into the autumn of 1973 when Aldaniti was moved there from Harrowgate Stud to learn that there was more to life than lazing about in fields. Some of the foals sired by Derek H turned out very sharp. Difficult. As David was used to dealing with them, he nearly always broke them for his father, taking them over to his farm while he did so. With two already broken earlier in the year, there was only Aldaniti left. David was a firm believer that if a horse was going to be a jumper, as they imagined Aldaniti would, then there were no short cuts to the job. He started working the three-year-old on the lunge as soon as he had settled into his new surroundings.

With his assistant Val Greaves leading Aldaniti round in a circle while David stood in the middle holding the long lunge rope, Aldaniti soon learnt that when David said "walk on" and flicked the long whip on the ground, that he was to walk, out on his own, round the edge of the circle, and that when the voice of command ordered "whoa", he was to stop. With Val at his head to show him what was expected of him, Aldaniti learnt quickly. First in one direction then, so as to avoid building up one set of muscles more than the other, doing an equal amount of work in the other direction.

After the first ten minutes David thought that the youngster was ready to try it on his own. "You get him going, and then let go and let him go on ahead of you," David instructed Val Greaves.

"O.K.," the girl called back.

"Walk on!" David's voice commanded. Aldaniti obeyed, walking calmly round on the loose lunge as Val gradually disappeared behind him. His immediate reaction was panic at being on his own. He stopped, turned in, and began to walk towards David.

"Whoa," David ordered, quickly walking up to the horse and taking him back to the track. "Walk on," he ordered again. Aldaniti instinctively turned in again. Once again he was led back to the outside of the circle, and led off by Val. Gradually he came to understand what was expected of him. The lunge work helped strengthen his legs and body before he was asked to work with the additional weight of a rider on his back, and as he got stronger, the lessons lengthened accordingly. Soon he was trotting and cantering on the lunge, on either rein, obedient to the voice in the middle of the circle. It was obvious that the youngster enjoyed the work, presenting none of the problems that he might have inherited from Derek H.

The next step was the introduction of long reins, one on either side of the bit in his mouth, with David driving him from a distance behind so that he would learn to go forward freely without anyone near his head and also get used to the guidance of the bit telling him which direction to take. The first walks were round the farm, inspecting tractors and other pieces of machinery, making left and right turns, all the time moving forward. When Aldaniti had understood what he was to do David took him out on to the roads where he learnt what traffic was like.

"He's just the sort of horse you want to do," David told Val Greaves, well satisfied with Aldaniti's progress after long-reining him round the lanes. "Takes it all in his stride."

Within six weeks of this work, Aldaniti had come on enough to be backed. He accepted David on his back straight away and in a few days was being ridden round the farm with the other horses. Schooling continued though, with basic jumping lessons on the lunge so that the big horse could learn to see a stride and fiddle his way out if he made a mistake, again without the added weight of a rider to start with. These first jumps were never more than two feet high, and right from the beginning it was obvious that Aldaniti enjoyed jumping, as he appeared to appreciate everything that he was asked to do.

Tommy Barron was often over at Northallerton, always interested to see how this horse that they all loved was coming on. "He's got scope," he said after watching him jump through a small grid. "He'll make a bit of money—which is what it's all about."

"He's always a gentleman, this one," David remarked, patting the chestnut appreciatively.

"Yes," his father agreed. "Not sharp like some of them."

"No." David laughed. "By the time I've finished with him we'll know that the next person can get on him and ride him—which is more than can be said of some."

Early in the new year when the four-year-old Aldaniti had been out with the other horses and had generally seen a bit of life, David decided that it was time to show him hounds. The ground was not too hard and the horse was fit.

"Just for an hour," David said to Val Greaves who was riding the chestnut youngster, while David himself was on an older horse to act as schoolmaster. The Hurworth were meeting nearby that day so the two horses hacked on together, their warm breath blowing out to hang in the cold air. Aldaniti knew immediately that this was no ordinary day's work. There was a freshness about the day, his mane had been plaited, and the old horse beside him was on his toes. Aldaniti stepped out keenly, waiting expectantly to see what it was all about.

Hounds had already arrived at the meet. About twenty horses were there, too, and more coming from each direction. "We'll keep them moving on the edge," David instructed Val. "How does he feel?"

"Fine." Val patted Aldaniti on the neck as they walked round outside the main mass of horses, hounds and foot-followers. Ears pricked, eyes wide, Aldaniti took it all in, the sounds, the colour, also the air of anticipation and excitement that passed between the other horses. When the Master collected his hounds to move off to draw the first covert, David and Val turned their horses in to follow at the rear of the field, trotting side by side, the older horse helping Aldaniti to keep calm. "That's a nice one, David," called a hunting friend. "One of yours?"

"Father's," David replied.

"He for sale then?"

"Will be when he's ready—at a price," David added.

"Not going to train him yourself then?"

"I'd like to, but I'm not," David admitted as he shook his head.

Aldaniti followed the field off the road and into a corner of the covert, where they were to wait. Having just got going and sensing that this would be fun, he was impatient at being asked to stand so soon. Nodding his head so that his bit rattled in his mouth, he pawed the ground. Val walked him round on the outside before asking him to stand again.

Hounds were drawing the covert, encouraged by the voice of the huntsman. People laughed and chatted, ignoring the cold. Horses touched noses and squealed. Aldaniti was alert, ready and waiting, but obedient to the order to stay still given to him again by Val.

One hound gave voice—a second echoed it. Within minutes the pack was on the scent, hunting in full cry.

"They're running out the other side," someone called.

Between the field and the fast diminishing cries of the hounds was a gap in the hedge filled with a post and rails. The first horse to jump clipped the top and nearly fell. Others got too close. Some stopped. Some charged with their heads up, fighting to be away.

"You go now," David told Val when they were the only two left waiting.

Val turned Aldaniti towards the post and rails. She felt him see the fence and hardly had to help him at all as he went into it, found a stride, and popped over. Without waiting for David, Val told Aldaniti to follow the others. He galloped freely and calmly, covering the ground with a long, powerful stride. By

23

the time they had jumped a small hedge and another post and rails, hounds checked. Aldaniti stopped with the other horses, blowing slightly, eager to be off again.

"That's enough today," David said to Val. "We'll go while it's quiet."

Reluctantly, Aldaniti allowed himself to be turned away from the others and the fun. David and Val were thrilled with him though. "He jumped that first one super," David said. "Believe you me, he was the only horse today who went into it properly. He showed them how to jump, and on his first day out."

Val kept Aldaniti on the bit until she felt him settle, then she patted his neck and let him relax on a loose rein as a reward for behaving so well.

Several more days out with hounds followed, never for more than an hour or two. Each time David could have sold the gelding; each time out Aldaniti thoroughly enjoyed himself without putting a foot wrong. Not even on the third day, when he knew exactly what was going to happen, exactly where he was going, that there would be galloping, jumping and other horses, did he misbehave or get silly like most young horses when they are introduced to hunting.

Having proved that the horse had jumping ability—as well as manners—David was interested to see if he had the speed that a jumper would need. So one morning, with Val riding an experienced and successful point-to-pointer, and David on Aldaniti, they headed for the long, flat field that was used for galloping.

"I'm just going to let him go beside you," David told Val. "Only for a couple of furlongs. Don't want to overdo it at this stage. Set a good pace and I'll see what happens."

"Right." Val urged the older horse into a canter—then a gallop. David kept Aldaniti tucked in beside.

"He's got the power, the foot. Everything was there," David said when they pulled up. He made a fuss of the horse as they walked back to the yard. "He's a natural."

A few days later, over at Harrowgate Stud, David told his

father about the gallop. "Will you send him to Doncaster Sales soon?" he asked, as that was where most of the Barrons' youngsters went.

"No," Tommy replied. "He's worth some money, that one. He'll go to Ascot Bloodstock Sales."

CHAPTER TWO

Will he make a racehorse?

Among the crowds at the Ascot Bloodstock Sales in May 1974 were Josh and Althea Gifford and father-in-law George Roger-Smith.

In one of the boxes, wondering what on earth was going on now, was the four-year-old chestnut gelding, Aldaniti. Not at all tired after his journey from Yorkshire, but showing his usual interest in life, he looked over his stable door, alert, taking everything in.

Josh Gifford, who had made his name as a jockey and who was in the process of the somewhat difficult change to establishing himself as a trainer, had in his mind exactly what he was hoping to buy: a nice cheapish young individual that would help fill the yard up as well as win a couple of races before he sold it on. When looking for horses it was normal practice for George Roger-Smith to join his daughter and son-in-law. They all felt that three pairs of eyes were better than one—especially when the third, father-in-law, knew more than the other two put together after a lifetime spent with horses.

They had got to the sales early to give themselves plenty of time. Neither Josh nor Althea liked to rush decisions when it came to spending comparatively large amounts of money on horses; they wanted to look at as many as possible before they made up their minds. George had gone off on his own in one direction, Josh and Althea in the other. They had not been separated for long before George found them again.

"Josh," he called excitedly, "I've just seen a very nice horse. I don't think you'll like him," he added, as he knew the type that Josh preferred, "but I think he's definitely a horse you ought to buy. I like him a lot."

The chestnut gelding, lot 115, was led out for them to see. "Look at the build," George said. "That make and shape: a good old-fashioned steeplechaser that."

To his surprise Josh *did* like the look of the horse. As his father-in-law had said, it was not his type. But there was something about it . . .

"He's got a good bit of bone," George went on. "A bit of size, too."

"By Derek H out of Renardeau . . . Aldaniti." Althea had found the entry in the catalogue. "Foaled 1970 . . . broken in autumn 1973 . . . had a few quiet days hunting . . . big quality horse with presence and potential." Aldaniti, his attention caught by another horse being trotted past him, stood bright and eager. "A winner in the showring," Althea went on. ". . . good straight mover . . . ability to jump."

"Will he race?" Josh muttered doubtfully. "With that pedigree there's nothing to say he's a racehorse." Aldaniti was returned to his box and the three moved off to look at another animal that, from the catalogue, sounded more promising.

"You certainly wouldn't lose money on that one," George persisted. "Even if he doesn't turn out to be a racehorse —there's always a job for that type of horse. You'd still be able to sell him on. Eventing, jumping. He's bound to do one of them."

"We want something that we can run fairly quickly," Josh hedged. "There's nothing to suggest he's even going to be fast enough."

After looking at one or two other horses, the party once again had lot 115 led out for them. He trotted up and down while they studied him, unconcerned, apparently enjoying himself.

"He seems a nice calm animal," Althea pointed out.

"I'm just not convinced that he's a racehorse," Josh said as Aldaniti was returned to his box again.

"He's a good sort of horse," George persuaded. "You'd never lose on him. He won't go for more than twelve or fifteen hundred. That's not a lot to worry about."

Josh and Althea were surprised at their father-in-law's persistence: normally he held them back from buying anything that did not seem to be exactly what they wanted. Still undecided when the bidding started, but with no other horse that particularly attracted him, Josh decided to join in. As Aldaniti was led round the ring the figure of twelve hundred guineas was soon reached. And fifteen hundred. Josh was going to pull out.

"No. Go on," his father-in-law pushed. "Have another one." It was so unlike George, who normally pulled Josh up and stopped him from bidding, that Josh went on.

The price rose steadily and again Josh signalled that he was out of it: too many people were interested in the horse and Josh thought it was just not worth it. "Go on," George insisted. Josh looked at Althea who shrugged: she knew it was not the horse they had set out to buy, but she set store by her father's judgment. When the horse was finally knocked down to Josh at a price far higher than he had intended to pay that day, especially for a horse that had no more going for it than its looks, there was a lot of doubt in his mind.

George was pleased. "Well done," he said. "Well done."

"I wish I had your confidence in him," Josh muttered as he went off to pay for what he was beginning to consider an expensive mistake. All the way home Josh remained surprised:

the horse had fetched a far higher price than it should have done, and he had been the one to pay it. The last thing he wanted at that stage was a large sum of money tied up for several months in a horse that might be better suited to the show-ring than the racecourse.

Aldaniti, unaware that he was the cause of so much concern, showed his approval of his new home at Findon by rolling contentedly—and repeatedly—in the bed of shavings that was waiting in his new box. The change of home again, the second strange stable in as many nights, did nothing to discourage his appetite. His feed was finished right down to the last grain —he had known what it was like to be hungry once in his life and had no intention of allowing that condition to occur again.

After riding out with the first string next morning, Josh had the new horse brought out.

"He's a good eater," the boy doing him said. That was always a point in favour of a racehorse. The nervous ones, the worriers, were often difficult to feed which meant that they did not keep the necessary condition that was needed for the job.

Josh nodded. Looking at the horse in the cold light of day, he was even more doubtful about what he had bought. It was a nice animal—but it would be some time before he was going to be ready to put into work. In no way could he be cantered about for a couple of weeks and then entered for a race, as Josh had originally hoped to do with the animal he brought back from Ascot. After a few sessions riding out it was obvious from Aldaniti's greenness that he was genuinely untried, certainly as far as racing was concerned. Once again regretting the mistake, Josh and Althea made the decision that the youngster could do with a summer out at grass before any more was asked of him.

While Aldaniti enjoyed the summer, resting, relaxing, growing both upwards and outwards, Josh felt the restriction of having so much money lazing about in a field. But he was a patient man. He knew that a four-year-old who had been in work since the previous autumn needed a break—especially if he was going to make good as a jumper. It was not a practice of his to push youngsters too hard, and he did not intend to start with Aldaniti—much as he would have liked to.

Brought in again in September, with Josh thinking of a quick sale, Aldaniti was fresh, and fat. Exercise, grooming and feeding soon altered his shape so that he no longer resembled a brood mare, and helped to bring him on so that he rode out with more skill and assurance. The improvement did not, however, result in a sale, although he was shown to several people. It was always the same old reason: the same doubts that Josh had voiced were brought up every time. Would he be a racehorse? With his almost total lack of pedigree there was nothing to suggest that he would.

"There's only one thing to do with Aldaniti," Josh said one evening.

"What's that?" Althea asked.

"We'll have to run him in a race and see," Josh said.

"Isn't that rather risky," Althea pointed out sensibly. "If he goes badly it might do more harm than good."

"It's a risk we'll have to take."

So a race was picked for Aldaniti and his training took a more serious turn. All young horses can gallop, but the galloping necessary for racing has to be taught to them, so each work-out for Aldaniti was aimed with that in mind: to teach him to gallop. The jumping involved, over the small hurdles, was not going to be a problem. The horse had already shown Josh that he enjoyed that, and had a good balanced style.

The nearest that he came to being sold was the day before he was due to make his trial debut on the racecourse when a client of Josh's saw him in the yard and was convinced that he was exactly what a friend of his was looking for. "He'll buy him before the race," Josh was promised. "He's going to Ascot tomorrow. He'll find you early on and settle it straight away."

January 10th, 1975 was one of those welcome winter days in the racing calendar when the ground was suitable for the day's plans to go ahead at the Ascot meeting where Aldaniti was due to run. No one did approach Josh to try and buy the five-year-old, despite the promises of the day before.

Totally unaware of what was in store for him, Aldaniti walked round the paddock showing his usual interest in any new surroundings, watching, listening, taking it all in. He was to be ridden by Josh's stable jockey for the past year, Bob Champion. Brought up in the hunting field and starting as an amateur rider, by then Bob was a professional with over six years of jump racing to his credit. Chosen by Josh for his particular skill over fences, this shy but reserved young jockey was especially good at introducing young horses to jumps and helping them stay on their feet.

Bob did not need a lot of briefing before a race. He knew what to do. "We don't know what this one'll do," was all Josh said. "Keep him balanced and keep him jumping. Ride like you always do." Wearing Althea Gifford's colours, Bob was thrown up into the saddle and led on to the course.

The start was the usual muddle when novices are running. Eventually they were given the "off". Aldaniti, keeping well up with the others, although kept at the back by Bob until he settled, took the hurdles as calmly as if they were the schooling fences at Findon. After the fifth flight Bob decided to see if the horse could give him any more. He asked: Aldaniti responded. Giving an impression of apparently effortless ease, he moved slowly up through the field to come in first. Among those he had beaten was the Queen Mother's good horse, Sunyboy. Several of the others had had previous races. Josh, all doubts gone, was thrilled, patting the horse as he led him in.

"It was all there," Bob said as he jumped to the ground, as pleased with the horse as his owners.

Aldaniti stood in the winner's enclosure for the first time, thoroughly enjoying the fuss and the praise as his saddle was taken off and a sweat rug thrown over him. He appreciated being the centre of attention as the crowds stood round looking at him: life was fun—and now he really knew what it was all about.

On the way home to Findon, relieved and at last grateful to

his father-in-law for making him buy the horse, Josh was thinking. Immediately after the race someone had expressed interest in Aldaniti. Not many horses won first time out: the horse had put up a great performance. He definitely showed promise.

One owner who had kept his horses with Josh right from the start of his training days at Findon was Nick Embiricos, a ship-broker with a passion for National Hunt racing, who also lived in Sussex, not far from Findon, near the village of Kirdford. Travelling home after work that night, he started reading his evening paper with the racing results, and saw that Josh had had a winner. Nick Embiricos had been keeping his eyes open for a young horse that showed potential as a National Hunt 'chaser.

Within minutes of getting in to Barkfold Manor, Nick was on the phone to Josh. "That horse of yours that won today," he said. "Is he for sale?"

"Yes," Josh said.

"Won first time out!" Nick was excited.

"That's right. Looks like being a good horse."

"I'll take him," Nick said. "Subject to me liking him when I see him, of course."

"You'll have to be quick," Josh warned him. "He's created quite a bit of interest."

"Valda and I will be down in the morning," Nick promised.

"Eleven fifteen?"

"Fine."

"O.K. Nick. I'll give you first refusal until then."

Nick Embiricos and his wife Valda were ready to leave soon after ten-thirty the next morning. "Josh said it was a good horse; one that I ought to buy," Nick enthused as he steered his car down the drive from Barkfold Manor, their home that stood in nearly six hundred acres on the outskirts of Kirdford, near Petworth.

"We'll have to see if we like him." Valda, always the more patient and cautious of the two, had been involved in racing and horses far longer than her husband. She knew that while she was going to see the horse because her opinion would be asked, if Nick really fell for the animal—and it sounded as if he had without even seeing it—then there would be very little she would be able to do to stop him. Even if it had only three legs.

Their joint interest in horses was a strong bond between the Embiricoses. While they farmed most of their land, they also ran a small stud, breeding mainly for the flat. Their four children, Alastair, Euan, Nicholas and Alexandra, kept ponies, Valda hunted, and they also had one or two point-to-pointers—horses that are hunted regularly before being raced between February and May—as well as hunter 'chasers that were trained and run from home.

Although he had not started to ride until his early twenties, Nick had played polo and hunted. Hunting had led to owning his first point-to-pointer and then from there he had graduated to National Hunt horses, seeing the ups and downs of the sport, the dangers, the accidents and the excitements, as a portrait of life itself in miniature. Born in London, his Greek father had died when he was three and his American mother had moved to Barbados where she owned flat horses—which was the beginning of Nick's interest in racing.

Valda, on the other hand, had been born and brought up with horses and racing all round her. It had been her whole background. Her father, John Rogerson, was principally interested in National Hunt racing and had owned the Cheltenham Gold Cup winner Pas Seul. Her mother, Eileen Rogerson, had been interested in flat racing as well. Eileen Rogerson's horse Salmon Spray had won the Champion Hurdle at Cheltenham and she herself had been the first woman jockey to win the Newmarket Town Plate—a flat race which at the time was the only race that ladies were allowed to ride in. Later Valda herself won it, becoming the first daughter of a winner. And their daughter, Alexandra, has hopes of becoming the first to make it three generations of the same family—but that will be some time ahead.

As they drove up the bumpy lane to the Giffords' yard above Findon, Valda could feel Nick's excitement. A new horse was a new experience: an added interest in life. The last string of horses were just returning from their morning's work. Josh jumped down from his mount and passed it to the lad who did it. "You made it then," he greeted Nick and Valda with a grin. "Althea's inside. Come and have some coffee."

"I'd love to," Valda said.

"Later," Nick insisted, looking impatiently round the yard. "Come on, where is he?"

Aldaniti was standing quietly in his box. While many young horses would have remained edgy and uptight, he was relaxed after his first day's racing. The lad stripped off his rugs.

He was not the sort of horse that Nick usually fell for, being slightly plain and heavily made, but that did not seem to bother him. "Won first time out. Nice, powerful sort of horse. I like him." Nick had obviously fallen for him. The horse appeared to be the nice potential 'chasing type that he had been looking for.

"Could we see him outside?" Valda suggested sensibly.

Aldaniti walked happily into the yard where he was trotted up and down.

"Moves well," Nick said, his mind already made up. He looked at Valda.

"Any filling in his legs after yesterday?' she asked.

"Nothing," Josh was able to reassure her. "They were cool. Absolutely right. He went on walking exercise with the second lot—perfectly all right."

"He's five?" Valda checked.

"Five this time," Josh confirmed. "Never done a thing until yesterday."

Valda nodded. "He's a bit old-fashioned. But I like him."

With that seal of approval the two men shook hands. "Done," declared Nick. "When do you think we'll be able to have a run?"

"Let's discuss business in the house," Josh suggested. "I think we ought to give him a couple of weeks to see how he reacts to yesterday," he said as he led the way out of the yard.

The four of them, Nick and Valda, Josh and Althea, drank

to the future of Aldaniti. The Embiricoses—in their different ways—both excited by their new purchase; the Giffords pleased that they had made the sale, and that the horse would be staying with them for the rest of the season and probably the rest of his racing life. With no problems arising from that first outing and the horse remaining calm, eating and working well, Josh and Nick planned the next outing for Aldaniti. The Panama Cigar Hurdle, specifically for five-year-olds, to be run over two miles at Wolverhampton on February 8th.

Valda and Nick left Kirdford on February 8th in good time with a long drive ahead of them, Nick already anticipating success as Aldaniti had been tipped as the likely winner in *The Sporting Life*. Their plan was to meet Josh at the racecourse, where they would be joined by Bob Champion, who was to ride Aldaniti again but usually travelled separately to the meetings as he lived in Wiltshire. This time Bob came into the saddling enclosure in Nick's royal-blue-and-white colours which he had based on the Greek flag.

Always tense before a race when one of his own horses was running, especially a new acquisition, Nick stood close to Josh while Aldaniti joined the competition already parading round. From his air of expectation and the eager way the horse walked round, it looked as if he knew exactly what was going to be asked of him this time and that he would do his best to please.

"There are some good horses," Nick said to Valda as Josh made last minute checks to Aldaniti's tack, notching up the girth another hole. Valda nodded. To her that was half the enjoyment of racing. Not just the winning, but the horses themselves.

Then Aldaniti was off to the start, and the three of them were left to watch, Nick slightly apprehensive, Josh hoping that Aldaniti's win had not been a one-off fluke. Once the race was under way Nick followed his horse move by move. "Are we in the right place?" he asked anxiously.

"So so," Josh reassured him without taking his eyes from the galloping horses.

As the race progressed even Nick could tell that although

Aldaniti was running well he was not going to win. Nick was obviously disappointed. "Fifth," he said quietly.

"It doesn't matter, he ran a good race," Valda said to cheer him up.

This time it was Nick who was not so confident, not so sure of what he had bought.

"You can't expect him to win every time," Josh reasoned as he went to meet the horse and Bob. "He's new to the game. Give him time."

"He's difficult to steer," Bob remarked. "But he went all right."

Later that month, on February 26th, Aldaniti was entered for the Orpington Novices' Hurdle at Lingfield. Again the different parties interested in the horse made their separate journeys to the course, Bob coming across from his Wiltshire home, Josh and Althea arriving in a slight flap at the last minute.

There were thirteen starters, all five or six years old, mostly more experienced than Aldaniti. This time Bob's plan was to keep Aldaniti covered, tucked in behind one or two of the other runners, so that he could not see too much of what was going on, and would be less likely to try and tear off without looking where he was going.

Aldaniti entered the betting at 3–1, faltered at 4–1 before settling at 9–2, two places behind the favourite.

Again, slightly tense before the race and smoking heavily, Nick was impatient at the delay while the horses were waiting at the tape. He breathed a sigh of relief when they were at last under starter's orders—then they were off, galloping up towards the first flight with Aldaniti well up, held firmly in the rear by Bob. He was jumping fluently, keeping his place. By the sixth flight he was making headway, beginning to improve his position.

"Do you think he's going to do it?" Nick asked excitedly. Only one flight to go and Aldaniti was right up there with just one horse in front of him.

"Might do." Josh too was excited. Rossini, the leader, hit the last flight. So did Aldaniti. Neither fell, but Rossini picked himself up more quickly and coming in to the finish Aldaniti could not find that little bit extra speed to take the lead.

Second. That was better. Nick was over the moon with his new horse. "Well done, Bob," he said as the jockey got ready to weigh in.

Bob grimaced. "He just didn't quicken at the end," he said. "I'll have to get him in front earlier. He'll stay all day."

"Only beaten by a length," Nick said as they discussed the race over celebrations in the bar afterwards. "He ran well." Everyone agreed. This new young horse was indeed showing promise.

Cheltenham on March 13th, nearly three weeks later, was the first big race for Aldaniti: with a prize of over £7,000 for the winner there were some of the top novice horses of that season running. Although Aldaniti tried his best as usual, and Josh considered it an even more promising run, he never quite made the front rank, and came in fourth, beaten by the good horse Davy Lad. Sunyboy, whom Aldaniti had beaten in his first race, got his revenge by taking second place.

The Embiricoses were not dispirited: the horse showed that he could race, that he enjoyed it and that he was prepared to put his heart into it. He was still relatively new to racing and had plenty of time to reach his full potential as he was still only five years old.

Nick agreed with Josh that it would not be sensible to do too much with the horse while he was still so young. So it wasn't until nearly a month later that Aldaniti was loaded into the horse-box again with the other Gifford horses that were running at Ascot. Also heading for the same meeting to race before him was another of Nick's horses, the grey gelding French Colonist, a hunter 'chaser who was trained and raced from Barkfold Manor.

Two horses entered in consecutive races had Nick even more uptight than usual, especially as French Colonist was always in touch in his race and looked to be well in with a chance only to be beaten into second place by eight lengths, leaving it to Aldaniti to carry the Embiricos flag that day.

The Sardan Novices' Hurdle, Aldaniti's race, was over two-and-a-half miles, the longest distance asked so far of the young chestnut. They were all interested to see how he managed as they were still trying to find the distance that suited him best. He tried but never quite made it with the front runners, although he satisfied Nick and Josh that distance was not going to be a problem to him by coming in third—with his old rival Sunyboy the winner.

Between them Josh and Nick decided that the youngster had done enough that season. Aldaniti was let down gradually at Findon, walking out round the village and roads. Then, on May 8th, he was loaded up with the older Weather Chart for the first visit to his new home.

To Beryl Millam, the headgirl at Barkfold Manor Stud, the big chestnut five-year-old that she had not seen before was just another young racehorse who would have to be kept in for a few days while he was wormed before he could be turned out. Her husband, Wilf, who worked the farm for the Embiricoses, had worked with horses most of his life and still broke in the youngsters at Barkfold. Aldaniti made slightly more of an impression on Wilf. "Those legs will never stand training," he commented drily as he inspected this new arrival. "He's stag-kneed."

Nobody else in the yard had heard that expression before. "You look at the way the lower leg comes out from the knee," Wilf pointed out. "It's all wrong—more like a deer than a horse."

Dismissed, Aldaniti was led into the box that had been prepared for him. Two other girls worked under Beryl, taking an equal number of horses each and sharing the care of the ponies and horses that were turned out. That evening both Aldaniti and Weather Chart received the necessary dose of worm powder in their feed, and were then left to themselves for the night with the other horses that were still in.

After a few more days of light work, Aldaniti was at last

urned out with the other geldings for his summer rest. Free to
oam and unwind, with plenty of grass, the horse filled out
quickly on the well-kept fields of Barkfold Manor. He was a
natural mixer, not inclined to kick or squabble as many horses
will, although he was often seen on his own, eating steadily,
slightly apart from the rest of the group. In the summer
evenings he would sometimes canter around having fun and
games with the other youngsters, while the older horses, some
of them pensioners in retirement, watched on. Then he would
be off on his own again, head down to the grass, to eat through
the night.

The relaxed summer days began to fall into a pattern for
Aldaniti. At least twice a day Beryl or one of the other girls
would go out to the fields to check the horses that were turned
out in case they had hurt themselves in the dark, or been kicked
by another horse. It was not long before Aldaniti was waiting
for these visits, trotting eagerly through the grass as soon as he
heard the call that always announced their arrival, as he had to
the Barrons earlier in his life. As his legs were checked for
knocks and bumps he would nuzzle the girls hopefully, bumping playfully with his head until he was given the peppermint
rewards he enjoyed so much. As soon as he knew that his turn
was over he would trot off to graze again so that he could be
counted as sound, content to be alone until the next visit.

Many of these visits were carried out by Beryl Millam. It
was the middle of the summer that she began to feel worried
about the newcomer. She was sitting with Wilf in the bungalow where they lived beside the stable block at Barkfold, when
she first mentioned it.

"That new chestnut of Mr Embiricos'," she said to her
husband. "I don't think he's quite right."

Wilf, who also watched the horses as he worked about the
farm, had not noticed anything wrong with any of them.
"Rubbish," he said, "he's just sleepy in the sun."

But Beryl was not convinced. For the next few weeks she
kept a keener eye on Aldaniti and made more of the field
checks herself. Several times she mentioned to Wilf that she

was worried until eventually she persuaded him to go out with her to have a proper look at Aldaniti.

"His coat's not right. It's too dull," Beryl pointed out as she tried to avoid being knocked over by the persistently pushing nose. "And he's listless. For a young horse, well, I just can' put my finger on it, but I think there's something wrong."

"I agree there could be more shine on that coat," Wil nodded. "But we don't know the horse yet—it may just b him. Or he could be bored. Some horses don't like doing nothing and he's been turned out quite a few weeks now."

Along with all the horses at Barkfold Aldaniti had been wormed regularly—a necessary precaution where so many graze. Despite rotating the grazing with store cattle and yearling lambs, the ground would always remain infested. Wondering what could be the matter with Aldaniti, Beryl ruled out worms. That could not be his problem. Equally well, although she could not put her finger on anything else she became certain that there was something the matter with the horse.

"You'd better speak to Mrs Embiricos then," Wilf suggested.

Valda and Beryl went out to watch the horses together. Aldaniti was eating, he had put on weight. To Valda the horse looked perfectly all right—but she did promise to report Beryl's concern to her husband. Aldaniti was brought in. Blood tests showed that he had anaemia, as well as being heavily infested with worms, despite the routine dosing.

It was not long before he was due to go into walking work in preparation for his return to Findon and the more serious training that would be necessary for his second season of racing. Dosing him again, the vet said that he would have to have a course of vitamin jabs as well as antibiotics, but that once the heavy wormer had taken effect there would be nothing to stop him going into work as had been planned.

With dogs of all shapes and sizes running in and out of his box, and several other horses in for company, Aldaniti found Barkfold a relaxed yard during his first stay of any length. In their turn Beryl and the other girls found this new horse a joy to look after; gentle, never bad tempered or bolshy like many thoroughbreds, kind and easy to do. He did not even object to the daily injections in alternate sides of his neck each time, although after five days the left-hand side of his neck reacted badly. It was swollen and stiff and too sore to have reins rubbing on it. So he was led out for the hour's walking work on his schedule. It was several days before he could be ridden again, and Aldaniti was a horse who enjoyed his work, but he put up with the restriction, showing an unusually philosophical attitude to life, totally oblivious to the extra work load he was adding to the daily chores.

As soon as his neck had recovered he was back being ridden again. Valda did not leave all the fittening work to the grooms, but took her turn at exercising with them. The first time that she rode out on Aldaniti she found herself in for a surprise. "I feel as if I'm perched up here in the air," she complained to Beryl. "There's nothing in front of me—his neck just falls away!"

"You do feel rather unprotected," Beryl agreed. "He does carry his head very low."

Apart from his awkward habit of walking with his chin almost resting on his knees—very much the position that he preferred when he was galloping—Aldaniti always behaved well on the roads. It was when he got on to grass that things became a bit difficult . . .

When the horse-box came to take him back to Findon on October 8th for the 1975/76 term, he was fully recovered, throwing himself into the more serious training with enthusiasm as if he knew immediately that the lazy days were over. He was a stronger horse than he had been the year before, every bit as keen, always trying to do more than anyone wanted him to.

No longer a novice as he had won his first race the season before, he would be running against a better class horse this time. Nick, who always liked to be as closely involved with his horses as possible, even when they were in training, got together with Josh to work out the best plan for Aldaniti. They decided that as he was still only five it would be better to take his training slowly, not to push the horse, so that he would have time to get really fit. Then they would run him six or seven times in the second half of the season when he would be six.

The first few weeks were confined to walking on the roads in the string of other horses who had just come up from grass to begin strengthening their legs, but also to get rid of the summer fat. Gradually, trotting was introduced, some hill work, and at last the cantering, galloping and jumping that he had come to love. On the Sussex Downs where Josh had his gallops, Aldaniti threw himself into the fast work, anticipating the thrill of racing again. Never satisfied with other horses in front of him, he showed that he had not forgotten that racing was about winning, pulling and raking, with his head so low that on several occasions he banged his jaw on his knee and finished the session with blood mingled in the froth that formed in his mouth.

Nick and Valda, watching him work in the early autumn mornings, were both impressed with Aldaniti's keenness and obvious pleasure at being back in work.

"He's coming on well," Nick noticed with satisfaction.

"Pulling hard," Valda commented.

Nick laughed. "I think he's always going to do that. He's certainly keen to go."

"You're quite right to wait," Valda said. "He's too promising a horse to rush too quickly."

Between them Nick and Josh finally decided that Aldaniti was ready to run at Windsor on January 1st, 1976—his sixth birthday as all horses celebrate their birthdays on the same day, New Year's day.

The horse knew exactly what was in store for him from the moment that his lad started to wrap his legs in the thick protective travelling bandages that always meant a journey in the horse-box. He was not silly with excitement in the parade ring, but it was obvious that his adrenalin was running from the way he walked out, picking his legs higher and throwing them further than he ever did when being led about the yard at Findon. His eyes missed nothing as, eager and alert, he fidgeted while Bob was thrown into the saddle to jockey him again.

"Keep him at the back and settle him," Josh suggested to Bob. "He's still trying to rush about."

Bob nodded as he turned Aldaniti to follow the others on to the course. The Touchen End Handicap Hurdle was a low-money race not expected to be too hard—just a round-off to the long weeks of training to remind Aldaniti what it had all been in aid of. He knew though, as he tried to fight Bob's steadying hands as they cantered down to the start. He did not need reminding.

It was a longer race than he had tried before but he came in third—a promising start to what looked like being an exciting season for Nick. Bob was pleased with him. "You still can't steer him," he said, "but he ran well for the first time out."

"What next?" Nick asked Josh when they were relaxing in the bar after racing had finished that day.

"He looks right for Sandown next week. Then I think we ought to think about some of the bigger stuff—weather permitting."

The weather, the bane of trainers and owners, could never be left out of the question, often losing them more racing days in a season than injuries.

January 10th saw the Embiricoses meeting up with their trainer and jockey at Sandown, with high expectations for Aldaniti's run in the William Hill Handicap Hurdle. Nick kept warm through nervous excitement, hardly standing still until the race was under orders.

It was not the success that everyone had expected. As soon as it became obvious that Aldaniti was running badly Nick began to question Josh. "What's the matter?" he asked, even more anxiously than usual. "He'll never do it from there." Josh, binoculars glued to the runners, could not understand why the horse was making such hard going of the race. "I can't see anything wrong—he just doesn't seem to have it there today."

When Aldaniti travelled in, a well-beaten sixth, Nick was really down in the dumps. Discussing the race afterwards with Josh and Bob, nobody could make out what had happened. "He just didn't seem to want to know," Bob said. "He hadn't any more to give."

"An off day," Josh suggested, trying to cheer up his despondent owner. "You know horses, Nick. Up one minute, down the next. He'll be a different horse next weekend, you'll see."

That appeared doubtful, though, when his lad found a little bit of warmth in his right front leg—off fore—two mornings after the race. He walked out slightly lame, and there was heat above the fetlock. "Must have been feeling it yesterday," Josh explained to Nick when he rang him up to tell him that Aldaniti was unsound. "It's only very slight. We've bandaged it with cold poultices. It's probably just a knock or a bang and he'll be all right in a day or two."

Nick and Valda went to see the horse the next weekend. "How is he?" Nick was eager to know.

"Much the same," Josh admitted. "Have a look for yourself."

Aldaniti was led out, walked away from them and trotted back. His lameness was so slight that Nick could hardly see it. He felt the leg. "There's hardly any heat that I can feel."

"I think he's strained the tendon," Josh said. "It's only very slight, but there you are."

Bleak news for Nick who had been looking forward to seeing how Aldaniti developed that season.

"It's no good kidding ourselves there's no heat there when there is," Valda said sensibly.

"He's shown us enough to know that he's a horse worth taking care of," Josh added. "He might come right again this time, but it would be silly to take a chance."

"He needs a year off," Valda said.

Nick had to agree. Basically impatient, he too felt that however disappointed he was it would be far better for

Aldaniti to have the rest. To try and go on working with him at that stage could well mean that he broke down completely, in which case he would probably never run again.

When Mike Ashton, the veterinary surgeon who looked after most of the horses in the Gifford yard, saw Aldaniti, he suggested firing both legs to be on the safe side. It was quite normal practice with racehorses as firing brought blood to the scarred areas which helps to tighten the tendon again.

Nick agreed. He still had French Colonist in training. Valda had Weather Chart and there were other horses belonging to her family racing that season as well. On top of all this, Nick had his business to run. He was a bit choked, but knew that Aldaniti would come back later, probably better for it.

CHAPTER THREE

Over the moon

Aldaniti watched longingly over his stable door as the strings of horses left the yard each day. He was led out every day by his lad, but it was another whole month before enough heat had gone from the leg for Mike Ashton to carry out the firing. This involved sedating Aldaniti and cauterizing both sides of his front legs with a rod, at regular intervals between the knee and the fetlock. The bands of fibrous tissue created by the treatment act as supports to the tendons at the back of the leg, as well as providing the counter-irritation which increases the blood supply and promotes faster healing.

After the operation Aldaniti had to wear a wooden cradle round his neck. His legs would irritate him to a certain extent and it would not help if he got his head down to worry them with his teeth. Many horses get exceedingly fed up and bad-tempered when they are restricted this way until their legs have stopped bothering them. Aldaniti, although he felt some discomfort from his legs, and found the cradle strange to start with, remained as gentle and easy to do as ever. He appeared to accept that he was ill and that fussing would only delay his recovery.

By the time the legs had begun to heal, it was nearly the end of April—three months since Aldaniti had last raced. It was still too cold to turn him out after a winter in, so he stayed on at Findon until the legs no longer needed powdering to calm the irritation and itching that comes after firing.

It was May 20th when the horse-box finally arrived to take him back to Barkfold and the inevitable worm dose that was waiting for him. He was still kept in, though, while the gradual process of roughing him off went on. At first he wore fewer rugs during the night and none in the day, and then when he had acclimatized to that, none at night, so that when he was eventually turned out he would not find it too cold. Each day he was taken for a walk and a pick of the spring grass that was coming through.

At last the day came when he was turned out with the other geldings. After so many weeks cooped up not even being ridden, most young horses would have gone spare, galloping about the field bucking and snorting. Aldaniti did show his delight at being free again. He snorted, gave one small buck and trotted quietly off to join the others. Beryl gave a sigh of relief to see him settle so quietly. "At least he didn't damage those legs again," she said to Wilf. "I think he's intelligent. It's almost as if he knows that he's got to be sensible if he's going to get better."

"Trotted away sound enough," Wilf had noticed. "But the longer they rest him now the more chance he'll have. I always said he wouldn't stand training."

That summer of 1976 was another period of relaxation and eating for the six-year-old Aldaniti. Fully grown, the good-looking horse made the best of the rich grass and the uncomplicated life. The flies bothered him as they did all the horses that were turned out, but he had his friends to top and tail with, when two of them would stand side to side brushing the flies from the other's face with their rhythmically swishing tails. In the evenings when it was cooler they would graze and

47

sleep and eat again, and on through the nights, their large forms moving gently in the dark in the fields around the sleeping Barkfold Manor.

Again anaemic, Aldaniti received more treatment, and each time that he was brought in for a night or two his legs were checked more thoroughly than they could be in the field. To everyone's delight the tendons remained tight and straight. His summer coat grew through where the firing had been carried out so that slight ridged lines underneath were the only signs left of the treatment he had had. As the initial injury had been so slight and his recovery looked complete, Nick gave a sigh of relief and began to talk about Aldaniti's future.

As racehorses tend to work harder when in a string, even when walking round the roads, it was decided that Aldaniti would start his fittening work at home—but only at the last possible moment when it was too cold to leave him out in the field any longer and he would have to come in at night whatever happened.

After a leg has "broken down", however slight at the time, there is always an element of doubt as to whether it will stand up to work again. Nothing was done with Aldaniti until early November when Beryl took him out for a short session on the lunge—beginning to work his legs without the added strain of the weight of a rider. Within a few days he was walking out on the roads, just for half an hour at a time.

With hunters to be worked as well as the hunter 'chasers that were trained at Barkfold, Nick was called in to help with bringing his horse on as soon as it was up to staying out for longer. Having hunted and played polo he thought that he would be up to anything that Aldaniti might have in his head.

There were six going out at the same time that day, all for road work. "I'll go in front," Nick said confidently as he mounted Aldaniti. He waited until everyone else was ready. "Come on then old man," he said to his racehorse—half expecting Aldaniti to think he was on the gallops and take off. Quite the opposite though. Nick soon found that he had to keep his legs working all the time to keep Aldaniti moving at all. Leading the way down the drive, he found it hard to believe that he was riding what Josh kept describing as a tear-away when he was in training. They turned left out of the gate, away from the village of Kirdford, for one of their regular circuits that kept the horses out for an hour. Nick kept after Aldaniti as the others were closing up on him.

He turned his head round. "You call this a bloody race-horse!" he shouted to Beryl. "He can't even walk he's so slow."

Beryl laughed. "He's half asleep," she said. "He usually is when he knows it's walking only."

A lot of racehorses go bananas after two or three weeks of walking. Beginning to feel fit again they tear round in their boxes kicking the doors and walls, often damaging themselves. The only answer is to start trotting, probably sooner than is good for them. Aldaniti did not bother. He accepted the slow work with his usual patience so there was no need for the girls at Barkfold who rode him out to introduce the trotting work before they were sure that his legs were ready to take it. He was a strong horse, powerful and competitive, but out on the roads he was never any trouble, completely unruffled by the noisiest lorries by then and not inclined to spook at litter in the hedge or sudden noises from the trees.

After his experiences of walking Aldaniti out, Nick had no qualms when Valda suggested that they should go off for a ride on their own one day—one of the rare weekends they were at home with no hunting or racing to occupy the time. "Aldaniti's trotting now," she said. "Beryl's got a lot to do today, and the others must be kept going."

"O.K." Nick was pleased at the suggestion. He and Valda did not often get out on their own together, especially on the horses that they both enjoyed so much. It was November, but not too cold, and for once that year, not raining. So at about ten o'clock Nick and Valda went down to the stables. Aldaniti appeared to be his usual sleepy self as they walked along the road, head down, with Nick doing all the work to keep up with Valda.

"I don't want him trotting on the roads yet," Valda said. "We'll take the track through the woods."

"Fine." Nick was relaxed, enjoying the horse, even if it was on the lazy side.

"You go in front," Valda said when they were on the grass, "and just trot him quietly. Nothing more because of his legs."

Given the aids to trot by Nick, feeling the grass under his feet and hearing the other horse behind him, Aldaniti broke straight into a canter.

"What on earth are you doing?" Valda called. "You're only meant to trot."

"I can't stop him!"

"Don't be silly, Nick." Valda, concerned for Aldaniti's legs, was worried. "Make him trot."

"I'm trying to," Nick called back as he struggled with the horse. He was worried too, but when he pulled at Aldaniti there was no response at all. Finally, by turning him, Nick managed to bring the strong horse back to a trot and at last, when he got back to Valda and her horse, a walk. "God, he's strong," a tone of relief in his voice. "I wouldn't like to ride him when he's really going—I can't think how Bob does anything with him at all." He looked down. "You don't suppose that's hurt him?"

Valda had had a good look at the legs and could not see any sign of trouble. "I don't think so," she said. "We'll have to see over the next couple of days."

"Perhaps he could do without his trotting today?" Nick was not particularly keen to try that again.

Not wanting to see either her husband or his horse disappearing into the distance again, Valda thought that he probably could manage with no more trotting. As soon as they were back on the road again Aldaniti immediately fell asleep, plodding along as if butter would not melt in his mouth. "You old devil," Nick muttered as he patted the horse. "Thought you'd got away with me there, didn't you?"

By the middle of December, as there were no problems with

his legs, Aldaniti once again returned to Findon and serious training.

Apart from being extremely fat, Josh was thrilled with the way he looked, especially his legs. The tendon was straight and cool. The horse himself had grown and improved to such an extent that it was decided the time had come to move him up from hurdling to the bigger fences of steeplechases. Knowing how keen Aldaniti would be to try and overdo things once he saw the gallops, Josh kept him on the roads for another two months. It was not until he was a really fit horse that Josh took the step of asking Bob to school him over the big practice fences that they had at Findon.

Hurdles are low, about three-foot-six inches. They also give way if a horse hits them. Proper fences are a different kettle of fish altogether—four foot six inches at least, wide with it, and they do not fall down when a horse takes liberties with them. Some horses do not want to go over them at all. But that was not the problem with Aldaniti. Too bold for his own good, the horse attacked them with his usual keen enthusiasm as if he had been jumping them all his life. Galloping in too fast, he made one or two mistakes, but never looked like coming down, or unseating Bob—who very rarely fell off anyhow. It was obvious that Aldaniti loved jumping and these bigger fences were not going to be a problem to him unless he got so carried away that he became careless.

As Aldaniti had come up into work so late that year, and then been taken on slowly by Josh, Nick had to wait until February 17th, 1977 to see his horse run again—nearly thirteen months since his last race over the smaller hurdles. It was Ascot, the Sapling Novices' Chase. Nick, fully aware of the dangers involved, was always uptight when any of his horses were running over the big fences. That day was no exception. Smoking like a chimney, he stayed close to Josh all the time they were in the saddling enclosure.

"Right, Bob," Josh said briefly to his jockey. "The thing is to get him round safely so that we can see how those legs stand up to it."

"Right Governor," and Bob was being led out to the course with the others, with Aldaniti obviously delighted to be back in action again.

Nick followed his horse down to the start through binoculars. "Why don't they hurry up and get on with it?" he asked Josh impatiently as there was the usual delay while every girth was checked and some horses refused to line up. Eventually they were off. Despite Bob's efforts to get him settled, Aldaniti was determined to show everyone how much he was enjoying himself. Some of his jumping was extremely erratic, which did not help Nick's nerves. Then they were coming up to the last and it looked as if Aldaniti was in with a chance. "Do you think he's going to do it?" he muttered to Josh.

Aldaniti had not quite got the speed for the finish and was beaten into second place by the very good horse Tree Tangle. Even Nick could not be disappointed by that. "What a comeback!" The delighted smile on his face told everyone how thrilled he was.

"He certainly loves his jumping," Valda said, extremely relieved to see the horse back in one piece. "He had his ears pricked the whole way round."

"Not a bad performance," said a delighted Josh. "Now we've got to wait and see how those legs react."

The three days after a race are crucial with any horse. For one that has had leg problems they are even more important. Aldaniti was inspected each day, morning and evening. When the seventy-two hours were up and the legs were still cool and tight, Josh called Nick to discuss further plans.

At Newbury a few weeks later on March 4th, Aldaniti was favourite for the Burford Novices' Chase. Nick's reaction was a mixture of delight and added tension from the obvious fact that he was not the only one who expected the horse to do well. From the start Aldaniti attacked the big fences with ferocious enthusiasm. Looking absolutely super it seemed that no one was going to beat him—until his eagerness led him to make a bad mistake at the first ditch. He was such a big, strong horse that there was nothing Bob could do but fall as he was virtually pulled out of the saddle.

"Can't be helped," Nick said, trying to cover his disappointment. "When's he going to run again?"

Josh was not so pleased either as from where he had been standing he had been unable to see any real reason for Bob to come off.

Eleven days later, March 15th, they were all off again. This time Bob had the shortest journey as Cheltenham was not far from his Wiltshire home. Aldaniti was entered in a big race, The Sun Alliance Chase, where he would meet the long up-hill stretch of the course which is considered to add an extra quarter of a mile to the distance of the track compared with courses on level ground. Although he had raced up it before over hurdles, Aldaniti tired visibly and scraped home seventh, which was considered a good effort in such a big race. As always, he had put his whole heart into the race, trying his best for Bob as well as Nick and Josh. Then it was Ascot.

The going was good to soft for the eight starters of the Heatherwood Novices' Chase at the end of the afternoon on April 1st. Again mentioned in *The Sporting Life* as the horse the others were going to have to beat, Aldaniti started favourite. Giving a superb display of jumping, he led the whole way to win by fifteen lengths.

Nick's pleasure was infectious as he proudly led his horse into the winners' enclosure for the first time. "Wasn't that super?" he grinned, patting the steaming horse. "You did it. I knew you would!" Aldaniti, still wound up from his race, pushed his nose into his owner, nearly knocking him over.

"He knows he's won." Valda's laugh was full of relief. She did not mind whether they did well—it was getting home, getting round safely that satisfied her. Once the race was over and she could relax again, she was pleased for Nick and Aldaniti.

"He certainly does," agreed Josh.

Four days later they were off again, with Aldaniti running in the Flansham Novices' Chase at Fontwell on April 5th. Again favourite, it looked as if it would be a battle between Aldaniti and a slightly younger horse, Royal Epic. This proved to be the case. "He's in the lead," Nick said as they landed after the fifth. Urging him on under his breath, binoculars shaking, Nick was sharing every minute of the race with his horse. Royal Epic took over the lead at the twelfth and despite some hard riding by his jockey, Bob, Aldaniti was unable to produce the speed on the tight track and had to be content with second place, beaten by three lengths.

There was one outing left that season, for which Aldaniti qualified through his sire, Derek H. The Philip Cornes Hunters' Improvement Society Handicap Chase at Uttoxeter on April 23rd. Starting as favourite for the third time running, Aldaniti attacked the fences as if he knew how important it was to more people than just his owner.

"Oh no!" Valda cried.

"What's happened?" Nick could not quite see, but the shouts from the crowd were enough to let him know it was something serious.

"The saddle's slipped right back," Josh said. "Bob's still on—but he'll never stay there." With a full circuit still to go it seemed impossible for any jockey to finish a race with a saddle as far back as that.

Bob hung on with everything he'd got as the saddle slipped around underneath him. Half-way round Aldaniti was lying third—still with a jockey on top. By the tenth he was in the lead, ploughing through the last two fences to groans from the crowd who expected him or his jockey to go down each time, but he galloped on to amaze them all and to win by five lengths.

The cries of delight from his home party were lost in the roars of approval from the crowd. In the winners' enclosure Bob admitted to being as amazed as everyone else that he had stayed on. "I just couldn't ride him by the end," he said. Aldaniti was unmoved by an experience that would have sent most other horses crazy. The girth was up by his back legs and the saddle loose. But he knew that he was the centre of attention, and loved every minute of it, knocking people with his nose, standing alert, steaming—and proud.

There were no complaints over the seven-year-old horse's performance that day, or over the season as a whole. Having won two races and only just missed a further two he had left no doubt that this was indeed the beginning of a promising career—one that would be worth watching the next time he came up.

The few quiet days at Findon passed quickly as Aldaniti was gradually let down with gentle walking work around the village and lanes, until he was more relaxed. Then it was back to Barkfold Manor. He was a more confident horse than he had been the year before, a little bit more sure of himself now that he had found a purpose in life that was both demanding, yet satisfying. Aldaniti had more to say to the girls in the yard while he was kept in for the first few days; more to say to the dogs that he remembered from the summer before—and far more to say to the other horses when he was at last turned out.

As soon as he was loose in the field Aldaniti was off. Kicking and bucking with delight he charged amongst the others until all the geldings were careering round the grass like wild things. "At least there's nothing wrong with him this time," the girls thought as they watched the seven-year-old, remembering the summer before when he had been fired.

Almost as if he was trying to tell the other horses how much he enjoyed racing and yet how glad he was to be back at Barkfold to unwind and enjoy the summer, Aldaniti played on and on. One by one the older horses dropped out of the game and returned to their grazing. But Aldaniti could not stop —too much had happened in the last six months. With the May sun on his back and the feeling of spring all around him, he wanted to enjoy the power of his legs unhindered by any rider, to test his speed on his own.

Eventually he slowed to a walk, snatching at the new sweet grass as he still moved restlessly about. He struck the grass with his front leg as if he wanted to dig a hole. Turning, he pawed again with the other leg, tearing up the grass. Continually turning in ever decreasing circles he lowered himself to the ground with a deep grunt of pure joy before turning on to his back. With all four legs waving to the sky he rubbed first one side of his neck, then the other, deep into the ground. Then throwing himself right over, he revelled in the freedom of a summer out and rolled away all the months of being kept rugged-up in a stable.

Aldaniti went up and down into the grass again and again. Finally, when all the cobwebs had been cleared away he rose to his feet and shook himself from head to toe. With a shriek and a leap, he threw his hind legs into the air and once more charged the other horses. Sliding to a halt, he put his head down to eat at last.

The routine of summer life at Barkfold continued with the twice daily visits of one or other of the girls and occasional chats with members of the Embiricos family when they went out to see the horses. Aldaniti looked forward to hearing their calls, and would heave his increasingly portly belly into action as he trotted to see who it was, nosing and poking for the treats and Polos that they always had ready for him. Of all the racehorses turned out there, it seemed that Aldaniti was the one who enjoyed human company the most, at times preferring it to that of his own kind.

"It looks as if he's actually going to have a summer with nothing wrong for once," Beryl said to her husband Wilf one night.

Almost as if she had been tempting fate when she spoke, it was only a few mornings later that Beryl went out to the field and was surprised not to be greeted by the friendly chestnut. Looking round she spotted him standing by the furthest fence, his head dropped, one side covered in blood. She caught him up and, talking quietly and non-stop, led him towards the yard. "It'll be all right." She tried to reassure herself as much as the obviously unhappy horse. "Don't worry, I'll soon have you feeling better."

When the other girls saw the state that Aldaniti was in they ran to help. "Warm water with salt," Beryl said as she led the injured horse into one of the empty boxes. "And plenty of cotton wool."

Aldaniti stood patiently while the blood was bathed away. Despite the pain he kept his head low, never trying to pull away. When the worst of the blood had gone, a long cut showed underneath the eye, right above the high point of the cheek bone. Blood was still seeping out.

"It looks as if it's missed the eye itself," Beryl said hopefully. Then to her assistant, Pat Storch, "You keep bathing that. I'll buzz Mrs Embiricos and ring the vet."

Alexandra Embiricos, nine years old and pony mad, went out to the stables with her mother when the vet, Mike Ashton, arrived. She did not have much to do with her parents' racehorses, but when she saw the cut on Aldaniti's face and the closed-up eye she was as concerned as she would have been had it been her own pony standing there.

"I can't put stitches in," Mike Ashton said as he studied the cut. "It's much too near the bone. It'll be a matter of keeping him in and keeping the wound clean," he instructed Pat, who 'did' Aldaniti. With an anti-tetanus jab in one side of his neck and antibiotics in the other, Aldaniti looked sadder than ever. "At least it's missed the eye," the vet said as he handed over cream and washes for dressing the cut. "I'll be back to see him tomorrow."

"He does look unhappy," Alexandra said as Beryl turned him loose and shut the door of the box. "I'll come and see him again later."

"He'd like that," Beryl said.

During the next few days that Aldaniti had to stay in while the swelling over his eye went down and the long cut gradually began to heal, Alexandra spent as much time with him as she could. Normally she was not allowed into the boxes with the racehorses—they could be unreliable and tricky, especially with children about. But Aldaniti seemed to realise that he had to be extra gentle with this small person who patted him and talked to him—and stuffed him with Polos.

The first few times they were in the stable together Beryl

Millam made sure that she was there too, just in case. But it
soon became obvious that there was no need for her to worry.
Alexandra was as safe with Aldaniti as she was with her own
12.2 hh pony. Encouraged to do any stable chores that she
could manage, Alexandra was soon trying to brush over the
big horse, and groom his tail—at least, the parts she could
reach. By the end of the week, as the cut had closed considerably and there was no sign of any infection setting in, it was
decided that Aldaniti could go back to his friends in the field.

"I'll miss him," Alexandra said sadly.

"Yes," Beryl agreed. "We all will. You mustn't try and go
and see him in the field unless you are with someone," she
warned the child. "Not all the horses are as kind as Aldaniti.
Come on, cheer up. Why don't you lead him out?"

"Can I?" Alexandra's face lit up as Beryl handed her the
rope. Cautiously to start with she led the big horse into the
sunshine of the yard. With Beryl beside them, and the racehorse towering above her, Alexandra led him down the track
to his field and watched as he once again exuberantly
announced his return to his other friends with a squeal.
Bucking with delight he tore across the ground before dropping down to roll. Alexandra stayed beside the gate watching
him. She had three older brothers, her own pony, but now she
had a new friend of her own as well. A racehorse, one of her
father's, that was friendly and easy and shared her taste in
Polos.

When Aldaniti was brought in again, earlier than usual as
there were plans to run him before Christmas that year,
Alexandra was still on holiday and spending most of her time
in the stables. The cut had healed cleanly, although the scar
was to remain with him for life. In his usual way Aldaniti
quickly adapted to the few days of indoor life and preliminary
work at Barkfold as if he knew that he would soon be off to
Findon and the other life that he loved so much. He remembered Alexandra and nuzzled her affectionately with his ever
busy, enquiring nose.

He was very fat from the summer grass when the horse-box

came to take him away. "They'll soon get that tum off you," Beryl laughed as she led him up the ramp. Alexandra was with her and together they watched the lorry leave.

"It'll be a good six months before we see him again," Beryl said. "He's got a long season ahead of him."

"Will you miss him too?" the girl asked.

Beryl nodded. There were a lot of other horses that she liked at Barkfold, all different, all there for her to look after. She was not a believer in having favourites when it came to looking after animals—although she was beginning to feel that Aldaniti had broken through that resolve purely because of his pleasant nature and easy manners. "Yes," she replied, admitting for the first time how much she did like the big chestnut. "It would be nice if they were all so generous."

Now a handicapped 'chaser, as he had won a novice race the season before, Aldaniti would be meeting stiffer competition than before. With no problems from his legs to worry about or slow down training, he was slimmer and fit enough to run at Leicester on November 14th where he was entered for the Leicestershire Fox Handicap Chase to be run over two-and-a-half miles.

Nick was tied up with business commitments. As Valda did not enjoy going to the races alone, but wanted one of them to be there for Aldaniti, she had asked her friend, Meg Martens, to go with her. Although Meg knew little about racing, she enjoyed these outings with Valda. As it so often happened that when the two friends were together whichever horse they were supporting had a good day, Valda had begun to call Meg her "lucky mascot".

That day, as it was Aldaniti's first outing after the summer off, as well as the first time that he was running under the weight assessed for him by the handicapper, Valda did not really expect the horse to do particularly well, although she was sure that as she had Meg with her he would do better than if she had gone on her own.

There was no doubt that Aldaniti himself was pleased to be back on the racecourse. "Look at him walking round like that showing off," Valda laughed to Meg. "Anyone would think that he's already won the race!"

Aldaniti had every right to walk out and show himself off to the crowds round the parade ring. He was the 7–2 favourite for the race out of a field of six, and he had every intention of going out—once things got going—and thoroughly enjoying himself. That was what his life was about, after all. He was slightly impatient as Bob Champion was thrown up into the saddle, sidling and trying to hurry things up. Once Bob was settled Aldaniti marched off, dragging the lad who was meant to be leading him, determined not to be left behind. Once free he cantered down to the start, struggling as usual against the restrictions that his jockey imposed, fighting for his head, pulling like a train.

From the start of the race Aldaniti showed no signs of having forgotten anything about his job during his rest. He attacked the fences with his usual enjoyment and style, eating them up. By the eighth he was close up with the leaders and never looked like being beaten.

It was a proud horse that followed Valda into the winners' enclosure again—walking with the air of one who knew he had the right to be there and should always be there.

"A four length win." Josh patted the horse.

"I must bring Meg more often," Valda said. "She's luckier than Nick."

"You may have a point there," Josh laughed, delighted with the way Aldaniti had run. "But Nick will be choked he missed this one."

"That horse'll stay all day," Bob said when he came back from weighing in. "You know, Governor," he added to Josh before he disappeared to change his colours for another race, "I reckon Aldaniti is going to win a Grand National one day!"

"I'm not sure," Josh said doubtfully. "I think his jumping is too erratic—he's too free, and that's careless. You won't find a careless horse winning the National. He's got to learn a lot if he's ever going to get to Aintree."

Valda had heard Bob's remark, and when she was reporting

on the race that evening, fence by fence, stride by stride, to her husband who was disappointed that he had been unable to see his horse's first success of the season, she told him what the jockey had said.

Nick shrugged. "It was nice of Bob to say that about the horse—it's a maybe, perhaps. A long way off yet."

Valda agreed. Nick was quiet. Like most National Hunt owners he had a big ambition to win the National, although he kept it to himself. It went back to when he was a teenager living in Virginia with his mother. He had made great friends with Tommy Smith who later came over to England in 1965 and won the National with Jay Trump. Nick had been up at Aintree to watch and thought that it would be smashing if one day it could be him leading in the winner. Leading being the important part. Nick never had the ambition to ride those fences himself.

"Would Aldaniti really be the horse to do it for me?" he wondered. Then he tried to laugh it away. "It's like an impossible dream. Bob was just being kind." But the next time he saw Aldaniti, he gave him a closer look. The idea had been kindled . . .

That win at Leicester had convinced Josh that Aldaniti should try for the Hennessy Cognac Gold Cup Handicap Chase to be run at Newbury three weeks later. Nick was right behind the idea. Handicapped to carry ten stone exactly, a weight that was impossible for Bob to meet however much wasting he went through, Josh thought that it would be safer if Aldaniti was ridden by a lighter jockey. Weight had become Bob's biggest problem, as happened with many of the more experienced jump jockeys. Despite wasting, and hours spent in saunas, ten stone was well below his limit. But Nick would not hear of a replacement. He felt that Bob's knowledge and horsemanship, on top of his already established relationship with Aldaniti, would more than compensate for any extra weight the horse would have to carry, and live weight, human weight that moved around, was nothing like as tiring for a horse to carry as the dead weight of lead stuffed into place under the saddle. Bob had partnered the horse every time out; Nick had no complaints.

Ten stone six pounds was the lowest weight that Bob thought he could reach, as it had to include his saddle as well as himself and his clothes. He made it on the morning of the race as promised—just. Aldaniti was in fine form, excited by the journey, pleased to find a racecourse at the other end, not Barkfold. Determined not to let Aldaniti rush away too soon, Bob held him well into the rear of the field after the start, going well over the first and galloping on to the second. He landed smoothly, then was nearly brought down by another horse—almost losing his hind legs completely. There were gasps from the crowd as Aldaniti skidded along the ground looking as if he must fall. Nick sucked his breath through his teeth. But Bob sat still so that his body weight did not interfere with Aldaniti's natural sense of balance and survival. The horse struggled—and swayed—and made it to his feet with his jockey still in the saddle.

The rest of the field were at least a fence away, racing well. Expecting Aldaniti to have given himself a bit of a fright Bob decided to pop him over the next jump to restore his confidence, then call it a day. But Aldaniti took the fence well. Bob thought that they might as well hack round to the end of the first circuit and then wait there to see the end of the race. With each jump of this schooling session Aldaniti was making up ground. When they reached the point where Bob had intended to stop he could see that they were almost back in the race.

Gradually they crept up on the others with Aldaniti's extravagant jump eating up yards each time he took off. Coming into the last he had a real chance. There were only three horses in it—and Aldaniti was one of them. He could not quite make it though, and was beaten into third place by a neck and three lengths by Bachelors Hall and Fort Devon.

The display of courage and ability shown by his horse had Nick on top of the world. "What a run!" he grinned enthusiastically. "That was fantastic." He hardly noticed that Bob was in trouble with the stewards. Aldaniti's performance had shown that the horse did indeed have the kind of potential that he had hardly dared to hope for.

Bob's appearance before the stewards was due to the fact that he had weighed in after the race several pounds heavier than he had started out. Once he had explained that he had drunk a cup of tea to keep out the cold after he had weighed out while he was waiting for the race to take place, he was allowed to go—leaving the stewards to investigate, quite seriously, exactly how much one cup of tea could alter a person's weight.

It did nothing to damage Aldaniti's impressive achievement. In a handicapped race, one pound-weight is taken to equal one horse-length of distance, so for Aldaniti to have been beaten by just over three lengths when carrying nearly eleven pounds more than the handicappers had thought he should, meant that he had in theory won the race—by a considerable margin.

The Sunday papers were quick to criticise Bob's weight, Nick noticed the next morning. He was still amazed by the race as he read the reports. When the phone rang and he heard Josh's voice on the other end, he expected the usual suggestion of a meeting to work out the next outings that normally followed a successful race.

When Josh told him that Aldaniti was lame and had been when he had got back to Findon the night before, his immediate reaction was dismay.

"What's the matter?" Nick asked.

"Well . . ." Josh was hesitant. "It isn't exactly easy to say."

"Is there any swelling in any of his legs?" Nick wanted to know.

"Nothing," Josh said. "Nothing at all. Not even in the off fore where he broke down before." The trainer sounded baffled. "If anything he's lame behind. That's what we think at the moment."

"I'd like to come and look."

"Good idea."

"Valda and I'll be right round," Nick said as he rang off.

When Nick eventually found Valda, five minutes later but

in his impatience to be off it seemed much longer, she was as worried as her husband. Neither of them liked to think that there was something wrong with one of the horses, especially an unsoundness that had no obvious reason.

"Of course I'll come with you," she agreed. "I'd like to see for myself."

Nick was grateful. He knew that Valda had more experience of horses than himself and might well spot some vital clue that Josh had missed—although Josh was so thorough it would be highly unlikely that he had overlooked anything. However, if it was going to be difficult to diagnose, the more of them there were, the more likely they would be to get to the bottom of the trouble.

On the way to Findon Nick cheered up again. "It can't be anything too bad," he said to Valda, "not after the way he ran yesterday."

They found Aldaniti slightly lame, but as Josh had said, where he was lame was not so easy to say. Somewhere behind was the first impression, but unsoundness at the back of a horse is always difficult to pinpoint. There was no swelling or heat in either leg to indicate a trouble spot, or to help say what exactly was wrong. Nick, not prepared to take risks with any of his horses, said that he wanted Aldaniti seen by the vet.

To start with Mike Ashton thought that Aldaniti had strained his back—probably during the near fall at the beginning of the race. "I don't think it's anything serious at all," he said. "If it was he would never have finished the race. Lead him out quietly for a few days," he advised. "Just see how he goes."

Relieved again, Nick and Valda went home. At Findon Aldaniti was led out each day, still slightly lame but no worse and with no other sign showing to indicate that the source of the problem was anywhere but in his back. Josh and Nick were in regular contact, both feeling sure that it would be only a matter of a short time before Aldaniti was back in action.

When filling appeared near the off hind fetlock three or four weeks after the race and the first hint of unsoundness, Nick called Mike Ashton out again. This time the diagnosis was not so cheerful. "We'll have to x-ray that joint," Mike said.

Josh did not say as much to Nick but he was beginning to think that Adlaniti was so accident prone that if he did recover from whatever was wrong that time, he would soon be back on the casualty list again with something else. The filling in the leg looked suspiciously like a fracture to him, although Mike Ashton, who appeared also to be thinking along the same lines, had said that it would be nothing too serious or the horse would not be walking at all by that time.

The x-rays showed clearly that Aldaniti had chipped off two pieces of bone on either side of the joint on his off hind. "I'm surprised there's as much damage as that," Mike Ashton said when he was talking it over with owner and trainer. "At the most I thought it might have been a very minor crack— nothing worse—as it hadn't responded to rest. He must have done it somehow when he nearly fell in the Hennessy."

It was a far worse accident than anything Nick had imagined —and right at the start of the season when the horse had been going better than ever.

"Will he come back to racing?" Nick could hardly voice his doubts.

It is part of a vet's job to be pessimistic in case the connections build up unnecessary hopes. "That depends entirely on how it heals," Mike Ashton had to say. "He must have at least three months in the stable before we even think of him doing anything again. If that had been found in a human they would pin the pieces into position."

CHAPTER FOUR

The perfect patient

Aldaniti had left Barkfold Manor two months earlier a fit and healthy horse with a promising career ahead of him. When he returned in December it was a different story. One Christmas present they could all have done without. Beryl, who had never had to keep a horse stabled for so long, had her doubts as to whether any horse—let alone Aldaniti—would put up with the three months' confinement that Mike Ashton was insisting upon.

"We'll give him the big foaling box," she told Lin Wilcox, the second groom at Barkfold Manor. "From there he'll be able to see whatever is going on in both ranks of boxes." The boxes at Barkfold were indoors in a big 'L' shaped building. The box that Beryl had chosen for Aldaniti was certainly the biggest of the lot as well as being the one with the best view.

"Imagine how we'd feel confined to bed for three months," she said to the other girls. "And he cannot even understand how long it is going to be for. Still, we'll have to try and make

66

it as easy as possible for him." She patted the large nose that appeared to be listening to the conversation pushed amiably through the bars of his door. It seemed inevitable to her that the invalid would become fractious. Then what they would do she could not imagine.

The leg had not been plastered. Beryl and Lin Wilcox had been shown by Mike Ashton how to bandage it with a padded support underneath the joint, and left with instructions for it to be re-bandaged every day. To stop the other hind leg from receiving extra strain through over use, that had to be bandaged too. With hunters in to do, as well as other horses, nursing Aldaniti was again going to put considerable added work on to the three girls who worked in the stables. Pat Storch, the third of the team, was as fond of Aldaniti as the others, and always found time to talk to him as she went past his box.

Alexandra was upset to see Aldaniti bandaged and confined. While she was glad to have the horse back again, she was sad that he was hurt and became as determined as Beryl, Lin and Pat that the big horse should not become bored. After school, whenever she could escape from her homework, she would be out to the stables to chat to her friend, trying to make his life more interesting. The rest of the family also found themselves spending more time in the stables than they had done before, talking to Aldaniti and keeping their fingers crossed that the two pieces of chipped bone would float back to their right places—his only hope of a full recovery.

With his usual ability to adapt and do what was expected of him, Aldaniti, who a few weeks before had been attacking fences on the racecourse as if he would like to eat them, settled into his new life as if it was quite normal, despite the rapid change from full work at peak fitness to complete rest, without the gradual slowing down period that he was used to. He proved to be the perfect patient. Where any other horse would have been charging round the box, or even bucking on the spot with impatience at this confinement, Aldaniti remained relaxed, calm and as friendly as ever. Even with his diet cut to the minimum of bulk food—hay and wet bran—so that he would get neither excited nor fat, he appeared content.

During that winter when he became eight, standing obediently in his stable, Aldaniti made more friends than he ever had done at Barkfold before. Apart from Alexandra, there were her three elder brothers who were out in the stables regularly during the school holidays and who also found themselves attracted to the patient in the big foaling box, stopping to talk to him, feeding him tit-bits and generally helping him to pass the time. Watching the comings and goings of the other horses helped to stop Aldaniti from becoming too bored as well, and he enjoyed the late Saturday evenings after hunting when there was more work than usual at evening stables.

As much as possible was done to make life more interesting for Aldaniti, especially when it was realised how hard he was co-operating. The girls cut up carrots and turnips to vary his dull diet. He was groomed more than necessary, although as grooming creates fitness in a horse this had to be handled carefully. He had his rugs removed at least twice a day, and his body gently brushed. Then his mane and tail would be laid, his bandages changed and his box mucked out.

He hardly ever tried to barge out—only once when he was left with the door open and a headcollar on, which to him meant business. When the girls were clearing out his droppings, or carrying in fresh water buckets, they could always leave the door wide open without worrying that he would try to escape—as long as he did not have a headcollar on.

Mike Ashton was a regular visitor to the Barkfold stables. With several hunters and 'chasers in work there was always one of them needing his attention. Each time he went there he would look over Aldaniti's door studying the patient carefully. As he saw that Aldaniti appeared content, the horse certainly was not fretting or worrying in a way that could damage the leg, the vet left things as they were knowing that with any kind of bone trouble in horses time was the best cure of all.

In this way the three months turned into four, and then five. With the spring weather outside, Aldaniti could get none of the sunshine or grass that he needed. It was Nick who remembered the saying "geldings are better for spring sunshine on their loins". He had seen a horse in similar confinement at Newmarket with a heat lamp in his box, so he bought one and suspended it above Aldaniti's box. The horse loved it. His winter rugs had been taken away and he spent long spells, several times each day, standing directly underneath the heat lamp feeling the full pleasure of it on his back, finding some compensation for the natural sunshine he was missing.

The spring grass was coming through, rich and good to any horse. Beryl and the girls began to cut Aldaniti armfuls twice a day as it would vary his diet as well as bring him on. Most of the other horses were due to be turned out as the hunting season was over and the older children away at school. Somehow, though, that spring there was always one of them that needed to be in so that Aldaniti was never completely on his own in the stable block, left without anything going on to watch. Children in the village heard that there was a sick horse who did not bite and particularly liked Polos at Barkfold Manor, and their visits added to the variety of each day and helped to keep Aldaniti going.

At last on June 1st, 1978, seven months after he had first been shut in, Aldaniti was re-x-rayed. It was a safety precaution really. "He'll tell us how he is himself," Mike Ashton said, "by how sound he is when we walk him out." The x-rays showed that not only had the two chips healed completely, but in exactly the right places, which was lucky after the length of time that had passed between the actual injury and the final diagnosis of exactly what was wrong.

"Are you worried about him coming out for the first time?" Mike Ashton asked Nick. "Is he likely to buck and play about?"

Nick looked at Beryl. "He could," she said. "It would be such a shame if he hurts himself again through excitement."

So to be on the safe side, before he was led out to see if he was sound or not, Aldaniti was slightly sedated. Once the drug had had time to take effect, Lin Wilcox was sent to the stable to fetch him, while everyone who happened to be at Barkfold that day gathered in the yard to see for themselves how well the horse had done during the seven long months of forced restraint.

He may have been a bit surprised to find himself outside again, but Aldaniti did not buck; nor did he mess around in any way. He trotted up the yard and back again, and then Lin led him back to his box.

"Sound as a bell," Mike Ashton pronounced to everyone's relief. "Don't be in too much of a hurry with him," he warned, "there's still time to undo the good that's been done."

Beryl was left with instructions to lead him out in hand for a little bit longer each day and then, when the leg had had time to strengthen a bit, to start leaving the bandages off as well. It was June 19th when he first walked out without any bandages at all and was still sound. By then he was used to his twice daily walks, eating and watching the life on the farm, so that when those last restrictions were taken away he did not get silly.

The first week in July, slightly sedated just in case he decided to go spare, Aldaniti was at last let out with the other geldings to enable the leg to strengthen through his own natural movement as he roamed—the final stage of the treatment. He did not play the fool or roar around as he had done before, but he did roll. Again and again, over and over, up and down, until he stood for a final shake and a squeal of delight before putting his head down to the serious business of catching up on all the missed grazing while he had been kept in.

Once she was sure that he was not going to explode with his usual enthusiasm at being turned out, Beryl left him to it and returned to the yard and other jobs. But each time any of the girls went out to the fields for the regular inspections Aldaniti was given extra checks. They could always tell whether he was sound as he still trotted enthusiastically across the field to greet them and stuff his head expectantly into pockets for the Polos that were always there.

The fetlock was still enlarged and would remain so for the rest of his life. As the end of the summer came near, with Aldaniti still sound, Nick felt able to begin talking about racing him again. His first approach to Mike Ashton was met with the vet's usual caution. "Don't put any pressure on him too soon," Mike advised. "Try putting him into work here as slowly as you can."

"Do you think he will race again?" Nick wanted to know.

"There's every chance," Mike conceded eventually, "providing that he never has another similar injury. You were lucky. If the chips had affected the actual joint, then I would not be suggesting that you even tried to get him fit."

Keen to get his horse up as soon as possible, Nick was firmly persuaded by Valda to leave him out while it was still warm. "Walking about in the field is working the leg," she explained. "It isn't long before it will be too cold to leave him out. Give him till then."

With the cold weather of October Nick was at last able to give the long awaited instructions for Aldaniti to be brought in. The horse's friends from the village were at the stables, as well as Alexandra, when he came in from the field. Plastered in mud from head to toe, with the beginnings of a winter coat, a long, bushy tail and his mane all over the place, he was a mess.

"Can I groom him?" one of the girls asked excitedly.

"Is he really all right?" another asked.

"Please can I do him," Alexandra begged.

Aldaniti, who had not hesitated when he found himself being led back into the stable block where he had been cooped up for so long, may well have wondered whether he would ever go out again once the door of his box had been closed behind him. They did such odd things to him at Barkfold. But when Alexandra—who had won the argument—arrived with his grooming kit to try and tidy him up he was the same gentle animal that he had always been, accepting the slightly clumsy attempts to remove the mud of several months from his straggly coat without the complaints that he would have been entitled to make.

Alexandra worked hard. It was a long job. In the end Lin had to help with the high areas that the ten-year-old girl could not reach, except when it came to pulling his tail. Then Alexandra insisted on standing on a box and doing that herself, afterwards saving as many of the long hairs as she could from the straw to hang proudly in her bedroom.

Once he began gentle work on the lunge and then out on the roads walking again, and Aldaniti knew that life was going on as normal—that he was not being imprisoned for ever—he perked up and became interested in life, especially work and food. Each day his hind leg was checked for heat or increased swelling, but to Beryl's relief—and Nick's when he went to the stables to keep up with the progress—there were no signs that anything was wrong.

By November 27th he was off to Findon again, almost a year to the day since the accident. There Josh was equally determined not to ask too much of the horse too soon. "We've got to get him virtually as fit as he can be before we start cantering," he said. "He'll overdo himself if we're not careful."

"When will he be able to race?" Nick asked anxiously as he saw that as the real test as to exactly how much Aldaniti had recovered.

"It won't be long," Josh assured him. "He's not a horse who needs a lot of getting ready, and he always goes well when he's fresh. He's going to be difficult to place, though. We don't want to put him in a race where he'll have to carry too much weight."

The ground was hard everywhere that year—an owner's, trainer's and jockey's nightmare. Eventually Josh decided that if they were going to try Aldaniti to see how he was they either had to run him over Christmas or they might have to wait until Easter.

"It's the King George VI Chase at Kempton on Boxing Day," he told Nick at last.

"But that's a big race!" Nick had every right to sound surprised. It was considered the second most important race over fences to the Cheltenham Gold Cup each season.

"It's a condition race. They'll all be running at similar weights," Josh said. "It's the outing he needs more than anything else."

Racing was as much a part of Christmas to the Embiricoses as the turkey and crackers. Getting up early on Boxing Day and setting off towards a racecourse was normal. And knowing that Aldaniti was at his best when he had been out of racing for a while made it more exciting.

The King George was a three-mile-plus race that had attracted some good horses in 1978. Aldaniti was once again visibly pleased to be back in business as he walked round the parade ring—stepping out eagerly, impatient to get going.

It was the fourth season that Bob had been riding for Josh, and their best to date. But Bob was still pleased to be riding Aldaniti again, well aware that the race that Boxing Day was more of a test to see if the horse had really recovered from his injury than an opportunity to notch up another win to his own healthy tally so far that season. Not quite knowing what to expect, Bob cantered his old friend gently down to the start.

It became clear immediately they were off that Aldaniti was not going to win. As Nick watched nervously beside Josh, he became more and more depressed. Aldaniti did not ever look as if he stood a chance of coming within sight of the leaders. When he finally finished sixth, well behind, Nick began to wonder whether they had seen the best of Aldaniti's racing days.

But Josh thought otherwise, and told him so. "That was absolutely fantastic—in a race of that standard," he cried. "If I were you I'd be over the moon with that performance. After all that time off, to do as well as that against that class company—well! That's what I'd call a great comeback."

Somewhat cheered, Nick began to feel a bit more optimistic. Maybe there was hope for the horse. After all he was only rising nine. Some horses went on for years. And the horse had come in sound, showing absolutely no signs that he had been raced too early, or the race had done him any harm, which could not be discounted. Gradually Nick's old excitement and hope for Aldaniti returned.

Instead of being able to go out again a week later as they all would have liked, Aldaniti became yet another casualty of the bad weather. The leg had survived the race, but Josh did not want to take any risks with the horse. Frost and ice hit the racing calendar that winter—it was also too hard for Aldaniti to do much proper work at all. Walking and trotting carefully on the hard and slippery ground was all that he was allowed to do. Even on that routine Aldaniti put twice as much enthusiasm into his work as most of the other horses who just became bored and dull.

It was January before there was any southern racing again. Aldaniti was entered to run in the John Bull Chase at Wincanton on the 11th, a long time since he had last run on top of the extended period of restricted training. He showed his disgust by trailing in fifth.

"He ran desperate," Bob said as he dismounted. "Really too bad to be true."

It was nearly two months before Aldaniti could run again, in the March Handicap Chase at Windsor. It was a long race over three miles four furlongs, but again Aldaniti never really got going and trailed in fifth, blowing hard, showing that he still was not really fit. That was March 5th.

Again Bob complained about the way Aldaniti had gone for him. "Just didn't want to know," he said.

"He's not fit enough," Josh said. "We've been able to do so little proper training since Christmas."

Valda looked thoughtful. "It's not like him not to want to try, even if he isn't fit," she said. "He went a bit one sided, didn't he Bob?"

The jockey nodded. "He usually does—but more so today than other times."

"Have his teeth been checked lately, Josh?" she asked. "There could be something wrong there."

"They were checked," Josh said. "But it's certainly worth looking at again."

Valda had been right—his poor showings had been partly due to teeth trouble. Aldaniti had grown a wolf-tooth—a tooth that comes up in the wrong place so that it interferes with the bit and causes pain in the mouth. As soon as that had been removed he began to look up again.

After the tooth and harder training it was a fitter Aldaniti who was to run in the Piper Champagne Gold Cup at Cheltenham on March 15th. The rain had come with its usual vengeance to the meeting. The ground had gone from "hard" to "heavy going" almost overnight! Regulars seem to expect that it can snow the week before, but for the Festival meeting everything will be water-logged. 1979 was no exception —although it did snow again on the day which only added to the appalling conditions that had to be endured by both spectators and competitors.

It was very much a family party for the Embiricoses as Valda's two cousins, Solna Thompson Jones and Dana Brudenell-Bruce, were joint owners of the favourite for the Gold Cup, Alverton. Aldaniti, with no form to his credit that season since his comeback was hardly showing in the betting at all. Nick, though, had a sneaking feeling that his horse might be in a mood to surprise them and uncharacteristically had placed an each way bet on Aldaniti, then became too tensed up to eat any lunch.

Both lots of owners and their friends watched the race from Valda's father's box. The Cheltenham Gold Cup is considered to be the Derby of jump racing where all the best horses compete at level weights without the interference of a handicapper. Alverton came into the last to jump it level with the Irish horse, Tied Cottage, who fell, leaving him to go on to a clear win. Valda's cousins rushed from the box to lead their horse in in great excitement, while the Embiricoses waited to see what would happen next. The second past the post was Royal Mail, twenty-five lengths behind Alverton. Third, thirty lengths behind him, was Aldaniti.

Over the moon, Nick rushed down to lead him in. Aldaniti did not really have the speed to be considered a Gold Cup horse—coming third was a bonus that made Nick think that things might really be beginning to happen after all.

Valda's cousins were surprised to see the Embiricoses in the crowd near Alverton. "What are you doing here?" Dana Brudenell-Bruce asked, thinking that Nick and Valda had come to congratulate them.

"We came third," Nick said proudly.

"That calls for a double celebration," her husband Paddy said, so carried away with Alverton's success that it was Nick who ended up paying for all the champagne afterwards! In return Nick and Valda were taken out to dinner, but that was a few weeks later when it was realised what had happened. Not that Nick was complaining. With his bet as well as the prize money, it had been a good day for him in more ways than one.

With Aldaniti entered hopefully for the Scottish Grand National, it was his form at Cheltenham that persuaded Josh to let him run. Nick's hopes rose even higher. If a horse can cope with the Scottish National then he is usually good enough to be thinking of the Grand National the following year. His long-standing dream was a step nearer to becoming reality.

"We'll give him one more run before we finally decide whether we go to Ayr or not," Josh said cautiously.

The race chosen was at Sandown on March 27th, the Alanbrooke Memorial Handicap Chase. Nick was in a high state of nervous tension as the race would show if Aldaniti really had returned to his previous form and also whether he had recovered from the demanding heavy going at Cheltenham ten days before. The pressures were on.

Bob played his usual tactic with Aldaniti, keeping him tucked in behind the others until he had settled down. At the halfway mark Aldaniti had moved in behind the leader, Strombolus—a year younger than himself—and looked as if he might stay there. "Will he do it?" Nick asked anxiously, his binoculars beginning to shake as the two came up to the last.

"Yes, yes, he must," Josh cried excitedly.

Aldaniti put in one of his extravagant leaps, literally jumping his way into the lead. Nick and Josh threw their hats into

Aldaniti at home

Above: Beryl Millam, head stable girl at Barkfold Farm Stud, with Aldaniti

Below: Josh Gifford, Aldaniti and Bob Champion at Findon

Above: Aldaniti and Bob Champion clear Becher's Brook during the 1981 Grand National

Below: Last fence in the 1981 Grand National – and they're in the lead!

Above: Aldaniti is led into the winner's enclosure at the 1981
Grand National
Below: Welcome home to Findon

the air, jubilant, long before Aldaniti had passed the winning post, two-and-a-half lengths in front. Almost as soon as the race was over, when Aldaniti was once again lapping up the praise and fuss that was always given to him when he was in the winner's enclosure, it was announced over the loud speakers that there was to be a stewards' enquiry before the placings of the race were announced.

"What's going on?" Nick asked Josh.

"Nothing to worry about," Josh reassured him. "One of the other jockeys has complained that Bob crossed in front of him too close. But I saw it—they were nowhere near each other. We'll be all right."

They were. As soon as the stewards saw a replay of the film and the incident in question, Bob was cleared of any incorrect riding, and Aldaniti was announced as the winner of the race.

"Well, Josh," Nick said when the day was over, "do we go to Scotland?"

Josh grinned. "Definitely."

While hopes were high for the Embiricoses, life was not so good for Valda's cousins with whom they had shared success at Cheltenham only twelve days earlier.

Alverton, favourite for the Grand National that year after his Gold Cup victory, came down the second time round at Becher's, and was sadly killed. The horse was not theirs but both Nick and Valda were upset by the accident. Right from the start of owning hunter point-to-pointers, when he was younger, Nick had had to face up to the ugly dangers of racing. His first horse, Sampan, had been killed in its first point-to-point. He knew that one moment the luck could be with you and you would be up in the clouds, and the next moment disaster could suddenly chuck you right down. The loss of Alverton was a blow to the whole family. But that was racing as Nick saw it—a small capsule of life where if you could put up with the bad you really did appreciate the good.

Pushing these thoughts aside was the realisation that in Aldaniti they might, too, have a National horse. His run at

Ayr would show them if it was just wishful thinking or likely to be a definite possibility. While Aldaniti himself would take two days to make the journey to Scotland, leaving Findon well in advance to give him a further two days at the racecourse to loosen up after standing still for so long, his connections decided to make a day of it, travelling up by air.

So the Embiricoses, the Giffords, together with Brian and Audrey Trafford and the Tyrwhitt-Drakes, clubbed together to hire a small twin-engined prop plane to fly them from Goodwood to Prestwick airport. Armed with plenty of champagne they started to enjoy the outing as soon as the plane was in the air.

Just as the plane headed out over the sea beyond North Wales panic set in when one of the women in the party announced that she was bursting to spend a penny. There was a loo in the plane, but the pilot was not too happy about anyone using it. "You can't," he called back to the passengers. "The bottom isn't plugged in. Do you really have to?"

"Yes, I've got to!" insisted the desperate voice.

"I'll land at the Isle of Man," the pilot suggested.

"How much will that cost?" he was asked.

"We're running late anyway—if we go down now we won't get there until the race is over," interrupted Nick, who did not want to miss his horse running.

"It's urgent!"

That tone of voice could not be ignored; a large plastic shopping bag was found and suspended in the un-plugged loo. With everyone singing at the tops of their voices while the men held out their coats and looked the other way, the emergency was over, and the party just made it to the racecourse in time.

There were nineteen hopefuls after a share in the £20,000 plus prize money for the race. For Aldaniti it was the longest course that he had yet been asked to tackle. Over four miles long, the Scottish National is not nearly as demanding as the Liverpool National but it is considered longer and more demanding than many other races.

Aldaniti took the fences in his stride, making nothing of

them as he kept well up with the others. Riding a "waiting" race, Bob eased him into the lead five from home. When he landed in front after the last it looked as if he had made it—until Fighting Fit, who was making a strong run behind him, ran away to snatch the lead on the run in by two-and-a-half lengths.

It was a jubilant group surrounding Aldaniti in the number two box even though he had not won. "He stays all day," Bob said. "If I'd put him right out in front a mile from home then nobody would have caught him."

"Don't forget that last year the horse who came in second here went on to win the Grand National," the Clerk of the Course reminded Nick.

Nick was even more excited. That had been Rubstic, coming in second at Ayr before his greatest triumph of all. "Right," he said, his grin even broader, "we'll remember that."

For the first time the slightly more cautious Josh Gifford allowed himself to admit that he, too, felt Aldaniti had earned his due and was now well and truly a National horse. His earlier doubts about the horse's erratic jumping were removed as the dangerous carelessness had disappeared. It was obvious that the distance would not be a problem, the horse was certainly brave enough with the heart to go with it, and as Bob said, he stayed all day. All the requirements needed for the race.

So the 1980 Grand National was definitely on for Aldaniti. He had the jumping ability and the staying power that the race demanded, and his jockey would be Bob Champion who had ridden the course nearly every year since he had been racing —with variable results. But Bob knew the course, and, like all jump jockeys, was keen to win.

Aldaniti had one more outing that season. On May 7th he travelled to Haydock for the Stoke Handicap Chase. As if he was expecting the big fences that he had enjoyed at Ayr, Aldaniti roared into the lead from the start, and when he found that the fences were smaller began to treat them carelessly. He slipped at the fifth, losing ground. Making it up again by the ninth he romped home to win by seven lengths.

"What a terrific season!" Nick's delight in his horse echoed the thoughts of Valda as well as Bob, Josh and Althea. For an animal who had started out in November as an unknown quantity after a long lay-off, then given two desperately bad performances before coming through to be considered a strong contestor for the 1980 National it was a remarkable effort, enough to make any owner happy.

Bob, thirty-one years old with over 350 wins to his name, was off to America for a working holiday racing, his normal practice during the summer. Aldaniti, after a few days of quiet work, was back at Barkfold for a rest again. This time, though, instead of being just another of the horses his status had changed, and he knew it too. Still as gentle as ever and as kind with the other horses, he knew that he had really proved himself to be the one that everybody's hopes were on at last.

CHAPTER FIVE

Depths of despair

While Aldaniti relaxed and put on his usual amount of weight that summer, life took a cruel twist for his jockey Bob. Returning to England earlier than usual to seek medical advice, it was found that he had a particularly fast moving form of cancer.

Falling in a race at Stratford the previous May, he had received a kick on one of his testicles. Although at the time it had caused him considerable pain it had not stopped him catching the horse, Fury Boy, as it struggled to get up, remounting and going on to win the race. For a few days after the race the swelling caused by the kick had remained painful, then gone numb. Eventually, when the swelling remained, Bob became worried. An immediate operation proved that the tumour was malignant. Before he knew the results though, immediately after his first operation, Bob rang Josh to tell him that he would not be able to ride at the start of the coming season. At that stage Bob thought that he would only miss a few weeks of racing, but felt it only fair to give Josh the chance to line up someone else for those races.

Apart from Bob's immediate family and close friends, Josh was one of the first people to go and see him in hospital. None of them realised how seriously ill Bob was, but Josh knew that the jockey would be thinking about his job, worried that he would be replaced. The last thing that Bob needed was worries of that kind. Josh was quick to reassure him that his job would be waiting for him, however long it took him to recover —although as the months went by, Josh became convinced that Bob would never make it.

Feeling perfectly well in himself, which in itself was part of the disease, Bob found it hard to believe after further tests had been taken that he had a particular type of cancer that would kill him in eight months unless he undertook drastic treat-ment. The treatment itself sounded terrifying. Bob was told that it would almost certainly leave him sterile, that his hair would fall out, that at times during the treatment he would be so ill that he would be unable to eat, and his resistance so low that blood poisoning was a distinct possibility. And worst of all that he would need a minimum of four courses—and probably more—of the chemotherapy treatment that was the only hope of saving his life.

By the time that Aldaniti went back into training on October 19th, fat, active and abundantly healthy, it was a very different matter for his jockey. Bob was at rock bottom, struggling through the painful chemotherapy treatment that was his only hope. Never having felt ill before the treatment, Bob was looking and feeling worse every day. As he had been told, he could not eat and all his hair had fallen out. His fourth course of the treatment was in progress—with the hope it might be the last.

One of the many unpleasant side effects of chemotherapy is damage to the lungs. The doctors treating Bob were very doubtful that he would ever recover enough to resume his racing career. Bob, who could not envisage a life without racing, was determined to prove them wrong. While Aldaniti became muscled up and proved himself to be his usual tear-away self on the practice gallops above Findon, Bob, in between courses of treatment, took his first ride on his niece's pony, Henry, and realised that he had a very long way to go to get fit enough to handle a racehorse again. Riding the pony left him exhausted and out of breath.

The goal of riding Aldaniti in the National had been the one thought that helped Bob to continue through the gruelling chemotherapy. Towards the end of November he had to go back to hospital to find out whether the treatment had been completely successful or not. The tests showed that there was still a danger. His body was still not one hundred per cent clear. Bob could either have a course of radiation, which would damage his lungs further, or two more courses of the chemotherapy. Not a pleasant choice, whichever one he took.

Having made the decision to return to the chemotherapy, Bob was at his lowest when he went to Sandown the next day to see Aldaniti run in the Ewell Handicap Chase. It was November 30th 1979, and Aldaniti's first outing of the season. Also the first time that he had been ridden by anyone but Bob in a race. Richard Rowe, who had been given many of Bob's rides while he had been ill, was to partner Aldaniti that afternoon.

Neither Nick nor Valda had seen Bob since the last day that he had ridden Aldaniti back in May. Despite regular reports from Josh, they were shocked. Huddled against the cold which he felt keenly, the chemotherapy pulling him down so that he had no resistance, thin, with a National Health wig under his hat, they hardly recognised him.

Aldaniti started favourite for his race; not a particularly demanding affair, picked by Josh as a suitable pipe-opener for the season that would be building up for Aldaniti all the time to the National at the end. From the start it was obvious that Aldaniti had come back right on form. He jumped impress-ively with his old extravagance, more or less giving a lesson to the others in the race. Well out in front he was hacking easily up to the second from last when he suddenly went terribly lame. Richard pulled him up and jumped off.

Nick was thrown from the sheer exultation of how easily his horse was going to win to the realisation that total disaster had struck. As the horse hobbled towards the waiting group they could see that he had broken down badly on the same front leg as he had originally in 1976. The tendon was so badly strained this time that his fetlock joint was on the ground.

Nick, Valda, Josh, Bob—none of them could believe it. In one moment their hopes for the National next year, or any other year, had disappeared. Whether the horse was even up to the journey back to Findon was in question. If he did ever come right there would be very little chance of him returning to racing.

For Bob it was the final straw. He was absolutely heart-broken as Aldaniti, who had been his reason for getting better, for fighting the chemotherapy, looked to him to be beyond healing that time. What he wanted most was to be a jockey again and to him there was only one way—to ride in, and win, the Grand National on Aldaniti. Trying to hide his feelings, Bob turned to Valda. "Never mind, we'll just have to come back together." But he did not believe it would happen, any more than anyone else in the group. After a pain-killing injection from the Course veterinary surgeon, the leg was bandaged to make it more comfortable for Aldaniti when he was travelling. Then another blow hit Bob as he watched the last race of the day—to see it won by a horse that he would have been riding if he had been well enough.

Josh thought it might be better to have Aldaniti put down. In his eyes the horse was finished for good, but he knew that the Embiricoses would insist on giving him a chance if there was one. They were that sort of people.

Nick and Valda, bitterly disappointed for Aldaniti them-selves, realised what an even worse tragedy it was for Bob. Both Nick and Valda had lost their mothers through cancer. Any thoughts that might have entered their heads about having the horse put down were immediately pushed aside.

He was a good horse, and brave. He had come through two previous periods of suffering—they could not give up on him now. They had to try to get him better somehow: Nick was adamant, for Bob's sake as well as Aldaniti's.

The immediate problem was the journey back to Findon. No horse-box gives a smooth ride, however good the driver. Aldaniti must have suffered agonies. It was certainly a very sad and sorry horse that hobbled down the ramp and into his box that night. Josh, watching him, did not think that Aldaniti would ever race again. He knew, too, how much that ambition had meant to Bob.

That was also the opinion of the vet, Mike Ashton, when he saw the state the horse was in. "This horse is the type that is always going to be suffering from injuries," he said to Josh after he had examined the leg. "Might be better if he was retired."

"He'll probably go hunting," Josh added. It was the most likely thing to happen to Aldaniti. Once a racehorse had broken down as badly as he had that time they often did come fit and would then be put into some form of less demanding work than the one where the injury had been caused. A National Hunt horse might become a point-to-pointer, and a point-to-pointer might be used for gentle hunting; the pattern always going down a step—never back to where it had started.

It was several weeks before the swelling in Aldaniti's leg had settled enough for him to travel home to Barkfold Manor. Everyone there was upset to see him back so soon—and again in such a state. Especially Beryl who was beginning to think that Aldaniti must surely associate both herself and his returns to Barkfold Manor with pain, as she was always supervising some kind of unpleasant treatment for him. To her surprise the horse never appeared to bear her a grudge, and seemed as pleased to see her that time as any other, pushing her affectionately with his nose despite the pain he was in.

The tendon was still bowed and painful so that any movement hurt him. The leg was hosed down with cold water every day and then bandaged with iced cloths to try to bring the heat out. By the end of December Mike Ashton decided to try the leg in a support bandage until it could be point fired.

Nick was about the only one who never had any doubts about Aldaniti's future. Once he heard that Bob would not have been fit enough for the 1980 National after all, Nick felt sure that the jockey would be cured eventually and began to feel a grim determination that the two of them, Bob and Aldaniti, would be at Liverpool together in 1981. It appeared too uncanny to him that if Aldaniti had stayed sound that year he would have been ridden in the National by another jockey as Bob would have been too ill. Sure that fate was playing a hand in the matter, Nick could see Aldaniti recovering—he knew he would. He must.

Valda was not so optimistic. Well aware of the dreadful toll that cancer can take on the few who do recover from it, she was not too sure whether Bob would ever be fit enough to tackle the National, and after seeing him so ill that day at Sandown she even doubted his recovery. But she had the same feeling as Nick—if there was a chance of Bob making it then Aldaniti would too; although the leg was so bad that she doubted whether, if they did get him to Aintree, he would stand up to the race.

Another member of the family who never lost faith in that happening was Alexandra. She had been an admirer of Bob's for a long time and the news of his illness had come as a shock. Aldaniti's accident and discomfort was another cause for concern. At school she started a fan club for Aldaniti among her friends and at Christmas that year she sent the proceeds and a card to Bob from Aldaniti, suggesting that he gave the money to the Injured Jockeys' Fund—at a time when Bob was nearer than he had ever been to giving up his fight for survival.

Having seen Aldaniti break down, seen the extent of the damage to the leg, Bob gave up all hope of the horse ever coming back again. Without Aldaniti to keep him going there did not seem any point in going on with treatment that made him feel more ill than he ever had done, and in the end would only promise him a possibility of life—and probably not the life that he wanted anyhow. For some weeks he came near to giving up the treatment, actually telling the doctors to stop once. As he wandered round the hospital trying to understand why everything was going wrong for him, he came to the childrens' ward. It was the courage that he saw there that helped him find the strength to go on.

In the New Year of 1980 Aldaniti was ten, standing in his box, his future doubtful. A fortnight later when Mike Ashton came out to see how the leg was the vet did not like it. Putting on plaster to act as a stronger support than the bandages, he said to Beryl, "It's no good bothering. We'll never get this horse right."

Beryl stood looking at the horse, feeling really low. "This is it now, isn't it?" Mike said shaking his head; Beryl really thought that it was.

"Mmm," she agreed, remembering the time they had said it before only to find Aldaniti recovering after all. "He's suffered so much," she added. "And this is the third time . . ."

While he was in plaster everyone spent as much time as they could dropping in on Aldaniti to try and make the time pass more quickly for him. Margaret Phillips, who "did" him, was always popping in for an extra chat when she went past in between working on her other charges. It was four weeks before Mike Ashton returned to take the plaster off, wondering what he would find. To his surprise the leg was cool and the tendon had fined down a lot. For the first time he allowed himself to smile.

"Keep it well-bandaged," he instructed Margaret, "and if the improvement lasts a week we'll point fire him."

It did. The point firing was carried out on the damaged area, then the leg was blistered and bandaged again. For a second time a wooden cradle was fastened around Aldaniti's neck to make it impossible for him to reach the leg while the initial irritation worried him. Within a few days he was being led out on to the lawn outside the stable block to pick at the grass, and eight weeks after the firing he was turned out again for his summer rest, trotting gently across to the other horses with no more than a squeal of delight, again as if he knew that it was for his own good not to show his usual enthusiasm at being turned out at last.

Moving quietly about the field, grazing, drinking, mixing with the other geldings, Aldaniti gave the leg the best natural treatment that it could receive. The gentle exercise began to strengthen the damaged tendon at a pace that added no excess strain. The morning dew held by the grass worked as a cooling agent. The daily checks by the stable staff found no deterioration in the leg—instead there was every sign of slow but steady improvement.

"He's the ideal patient," Beryl said to Wilf when she had been out to see Aldaniti one day. "If he does recover completely we'll have his temperament to thank. It's almost as if he knows it would be dangerous to play around like a mad thing as he usually does."

"He may get better," Wilf said pessimistically. "But they'll be mad if they are still thinking of the National. He'll never stand training again after a breakdown like that—especially with those legs. They just aren't made for it. It would be a waste of time and money."

By July there was every reason to hope that Aldaniti was going to recover. Mike Ashton was at Barkfold checking his patient with Valda, Beryl and Wilf. "What are you going to do with him?" Mike asked. "Let him go hunting?"

Bob had finished his treatment and was riding again. His first attempt on racehorses had not been successful as one of the side effects that he was still suffering from was loss of feeling in his hands and feet. Running had helped to get him fitter, but in the end he had gone out to his old friend Burly Cocks in America where he felt the sunshine might help. Sometimes work-riding as many as sixteen horses in a morning, his determination to get back to peak fitness had returned with a vengeance. He kept up the running after riding every day. It was in America that he had his first shave, and his hair began to grow back.

"What we'd really like to do with him is the 1981 National," Valda said.

"I think that that's the one race that he could possibly be got fit for," Mike answered surprisingly. "It's late in the season, he would be able to have a very long, steady preparation. He'd be a fresh horse and they don't go at any great gallop. It's the galloping that would do the damage, not the jumping. A lot of horses who have had sprained tendons have gone on to win the National."

Beryl and Wilf looked at each other in surprise. This was more than they had ever dared to think about.

"You'd have to train him carefully," the vet went on. "Don't think of running him at Cheltenham in between and don't think that you'll have a lot of fun racing him during the build up. One or two preparatory races are the most that you can expect."

Aldaniti was left out at grass as long as possible so that his own movement would build up the tendons again without any of the enforced pressures that come through work. By October 27th though, the nights were too cold to leave him out any longer. Nearly eleven months after the breakdown, he came in again to start gentle work, with everyone wondering whether he would be able to take it or not.

The first few sessions were walking on the lunge. Then began ridden work along the roads for fifteen or twenty minutes at the most, and always—to start with—wearing exercise bandages to protect his front legs. Every morning there was the worry of seeing if he was still all right—which he was. Valda, Margaret and Beryl shared the slow, steady exercise work.

The problem was to get Aldaniti fit and keep the leg right at the same time. Hardening a horse's legs is the basis of any fitness programme. In this case it was also the most important part, for if it was taken too fast, or the leg not hardened enough, Aldaniti could easily break down again. Not only would that be the end of any hopes of him racing again, but it would also have meant that the only thing left to do with him would be to have him put down.

Before long he was walking out for an hour at a time, enjoying the road work, riding more like a police horse than a National possibility—except for one habit he had acquired. In Kirdford there was a small garage. Riding through the village one day Margaret found herself being taken firmly across the road towards the petrol pump. "Where are we going?" she asked Beryl who was out with her on another horse. "He doesn't need filling up."

"To see me," said a voice from underneath a car that was jacked up on the forecourt. All that could be seen of the voice then was a pair of legs. Gradually Arthur crawled out and stood up. Aldaniti stopped beside him. Although not a horsey person, Arthur knew all the horses that were exercised through Kirdford and as he was always ready with pocketfuls of peppermints, he had become such a favourite with Aldaniti that the big horse refused to pass the garage without calling in to see what was going on. Aldaniti put his head down and pushed his nose firmly against his friend's chest.

"All right, all right," Arthur laughed as he wiped his hands on a rag. "You'll just have to wait a minute."

Aldaniti impatiently thrust out his nose again, but Arthur was ready for him and stood his ground.

"Here you are then," he said at last as he dug a packet of peppermints out of his pocket and handed one to Aldaniti. "And one for your friend," he added, handing one to the horse that Beryl was riding.

The two horses munched contentedly, soon asking for more. After he had had his quota of three, Aldaniti rubbed his head against Arthur as a thank you, and was quite content to continue the ride with Margaret.

Soon the bandages had been replaced by tendon boots, just in case Aldaniti knocked himself. After six weeks' walking, some gentle trotting was introduced to see if he could take it. To nearly everyone's surprise—except perhaps Nick's, as he had never doubted his horse—Aldaniti stayed sound.

By then most of the other National contenders were already racing fit and hard at work, far further on with their programmes than Aldaniti.

Bob was back riding for Josh after the summer in America where he had pushed himself to extremes to get himself fit. His successful comeback had amazed everyone. But there was one big problem. Bob had had weight trouble before the illness and the chemotherapy treatment had increased it. Wasting to lose weight by hardly eating anything, on top of hours spent sweating in a sauna, do not help anyone to remain fit, let alone strong enough to ride over jumps. Bob was finding it exceedingly difficult to strike a balance. On top of which his weight meant that he was offered fewer rides—except from Findon where he was still stable jockey.

Gradually Aldaniti progressed to longer exercise. Two or three times a week he would be out for two hours over Bedham Hills. This involved a nine mile round trip with a long climbing hill that made him work and use himself, strengthening the legs and building up the muscle all round.

Gentle cantering was introduced too. The weather was kind that winter, wet rather than icy, so that the ground was rarely too hard to make the work risky. The main problem was varying the work enough to keep Aldaniti interested. So several times when the hunt was meeting near Barkfold Manor, Margaret took him to the meet and let him trot along with the rest of the field to the first covert where she would wait until hounds started to run and then—much to Aldaniti's disgust as he remembered what fun hunting was from his days at the Barrons—they would head for home again. It did make a change for the horse though, and stopped him from becoming completely stale.

Whenever Mike Ashton was in the yard looking at one of the other horses he would take a look at Aldaniti. The legs were by no means perfect, but they were no worse than when he had started work.

Over dinner one evening at Barkfold Manor, Josh and Althea had the surprise of their lives. "I want you to have Aldaniti back for training," Nick said to Josh, as if it was the most normal thing to suggest. "Bob's been through too much; we're going to have a crack at winning the National."

"You're absolutely crazy," Josh said bluntly. "He'll never stand training."

"I think you'll find he will," Nick persisted confidently.

"I'd love to have him," Josh said, "but you're barmy. It'll be a complete waste of money."

Nick insisted, so on December 22nd 1980 Aldaniti returned to Findon. He knew exactly where he was and that being there meant proper work again. As soon as he was led into the box with its deep bed of clean shavings he gave a sigh of contentment and began to roll. Up and down, up and down. The lads watching gave up counting after they reached the fifteenth time and went back to their own horses. The only one of them who was not happy was Peter Double, who had been given Aldaniti to "do".

Unluckily for Peter one of his three horses had been injured and sent home to rest, leaving him a horse short. To him, Aldaniti's legs looked frightful—more like piano legs than those of a horse—and he thought it highly unlikely that the horse would stand any form of serious training, let alone a race. And like all stable lads, Peter preferred to look after horses that were racing and looked like standing a chance. Taking their horses to meetings was one of the few chances the lads had of a day away from the routine of the stables.

None of the lads had wanted Aldaniti when they heard that he was coming back. Peter, being one horse short, had to take him on. He found the horse easy enough to look after, as everybody did. He just felt thoroughly depressed every time he looked at those legs.

To be on the safe side, Aldaniti was kept on walking work around the roads to start with, usually on his own. Like many racing stables the Gifford yard had several "Saturday jocks" —people wanting to ride out but who could only find time at the weekends. The quiet Aldaniti was soon a favourite with them, many of them asking to ride him as soon as they got there in the early morning. Josh had nothing to fear from sending these fairly novice riders round the village on Aldaniti. If there was one horse in the yard he could rely on to bring them back in one piece however green they were, Aldaniti was the one.

Once he was ready for more strenuous work, still doubtful as to how far towards the National they would get, Josh decided that the only thing to do was to ride the horse himself from then on. Aldaniti had always been a difficult ride when he was with the string. If his rider asked him to canter he would try to gallop. He was always trying to do more than he was meant to, and Josh could see that if he was not careful the horse himself would be the cause of more damage and wreck all the faith that Nick and Valda had in him. If he—the Governor —was riding him and anything happened he would only have himself to blame. His one aim that winter was to get Aldaniti to the National.

For the first two weeks Josh also kept Aldaniti on walking and trotting work as he knew that the horse would put more effort into everything he did as soon as he was part of the string again.

The first string leaves the Gifford yard at 7.30 a.m. every morning. Aldaniti was not asked to do as much as any of the other horses. Josh was really using him as a hack while he supervised the others who were training properly. Gradually some faster work was introduced into Aldaniti's schedule, but only on days when the ground was soft, and absolutely safe for the leg.

The weather that winter was an added bonus. If it had been a severe hard spell it would have been even more doubtful as to whether Aldaniti kept going. As it was, with plenty of rain, he did.

Josh, who had expected the horse to break down again at any stage, was amazed at the way he kept going. The more work he did the better his legs looked—the less they resembled piano legs as the tendons straightened, the more hopeful the National looked.

He had devised a specific programme of work for Aldaniti, so that if necessary he would be fit for the National without a warm-up race. It was Aldaniti's trait of trying too hard, wanting to please too much, that decided Josh to keep the horse working on his own once he had reached the stage of faster work. So Aldaniti never galloped with another horse upside him to give him the extra incentive. He put enough into his work on his own so that he did get fit without the competitive element that many horses need if they are to work properly.

To Josh's amazement, the legs improved beyond recognition. They were harder, straighter, tighter—better than they had ever been.

The weather held and Nick was away on a skiing holiday, but he had such a firm belief in Aldaniti that he rang Josh and asked him to place £500 on the horse for the Grand National for an each way bet when the ante-post odds were 66–1.

That was almost too much for Josh. "Don't be silly," he said. "They're taking bets at 66–1 that he'll even get there, let alone win the race."

Nick would not be dissuaded, although he did not usually bet. He rang off, leaving Josh totally unsure as to what to do. It was out of character for Nick, and did not make sense to him. It was Althea who provided the solution. "Put half on," she suggested. And that was what Josh did, even more convinced than he ever had been before that his friend and client was absolutely crazy.

Aldaniti had been entered for two races in February in the hope that the weather would provide suitable ground for the horse to run in one of them. When it looked possible, and Aldaniti was still going well, Josh noticed that one of the races at Newbury was to be run on Friday 13th. That was too much. It would be asking for trouble—and trouble for Aldaniti would mean only one thing—disaster. So they decided on The Whitbread Trial Handicap at Ascot two days earlier, as like many people involved in racing, Nick was highly superstitious and had no intention of tempting fate further than he had done already.

Of the eight runners chasing the prizes, Aldaniti was the least fancied.

"Get him settled," Josh instructed Bob. "He'll want to go and could be careless. Keep him on the bridle and above all bring him back in one piece."

The strain on the watching Embiricoses was far worse than usual. Always aware of the dangers involved when his horses were running, Nick was far more wound up that time than he ever had been before. Winning the race was not the priority at all. Just to get round without going lame was the point of the exercise. But was that possible? Josh, too, had worse pre-race nerves than usual. He had told Bob not to give the horse a hard race, but was any race going to be too much? And Aldaniti was giving all but one of the others weight—and the one carrying more, Bueche Giorod, had already won six races that season so he was really race-fit. In agonies of doubt and confusion, he watched the horse canter steadily down to the start.

Aldaniti was impatient to be off. Once the starting tapes went up he fell into his stride, Bob keeping him settled at the rear of the field. He made a slight mistake at the last fence first time round, otherwise his jumping was gradually gaining him ground until coming up the hill and round the corner two from home he jumped quietly into the front and no one could catch him.

Nick, Valda, Josh and Althea—and Bob—were all absolutely thrilled. A win like that was more than even Nick had dared hope for. Back in the winners' enclosure after such a long time, Aldaniti was also thrilled with his reception. Everyone was making a fuss of him. He was back doing what he loved more than anything at last.

Josh had never been so pleased with Bob before. "You did everything right and still won," he said with delight.

Among the spectators at Ascot that day was David Barron who had broken Aldaniti for his father seven-and-a-half years before. By the next morning Aldaniti's price for the National had reached 33–1. David added his money on to the horse that his father had bred.

The racing press was full of the story of Aldaniti's amazing comeback and the superb race that Bob had given him. At Findon, though, Josh was keeping an eye on the leg. "It's the next 72 hours that'll tell," he said to Peter. "If he's still sound then, we're in with a chance."

Within the time allotted by Josh, it appeared that the race had done the leg good rather than harm. It was cool, and the tendon was tighter than before. The Sun Grand National was beginning to look a distinct possibility after all, with Bob and Aldaniti back together again as well; something that after that fateful day at Sandown only one person had really believed would happen—Nick Embiricos, whose faith in them both had never faltered.

A few days later Josh was on the phone to Nick. "The legs are fine," he said. "Better than before the race. Look, I think we ought to run him at Cheltenham."

Nick was taken aback—running Aldaniti again before the National was not something that he wanted to do. "I'm not keen," he replied, considering it to be a great risk to take when they had come so far and there was still some distance to go.

"If he beat those horses at Ascot he's in with a chance for the Gold Cup, Nick," Josh persisted. "It doesn't look a strong race at all this year."

"Really . . ." Nick hesitated. "I'll have to think about it." He had already come third in the race with Aldaniti. The Gold Cup was a side issue that did not interest him.

Normally, with a big race like the National coming up where his horse stood a chance of being brought down by accident at the first fence, Nick would have wanted to run him as many times as possible before the major outing to defray the risks involved—perhaps picking up valuable prize money to help cover some of the costs, and to give himself the chance of some success. This time it was different. All he wanted was for Bob and Aldaniti to be at the National together—that was the whole point of everything they had been through, trying to get the horse better, and keeping him better.

When Bob heard that Josh was hoping to run Aldaniti in the Gold Cup he was horrified. To start with he did not consider Aldaniti had the speed for the race. But that year, in particular, if his legs did not stand up to the race he thought it would inevitably be the end of his hopes for the National—the dream that had kept him going. Whether the horse ran in the Gold Cup or not was not a matter that he could interfere in—he just had to sit it out, waiting for the decision that he wanted, worrying that Josh would win the argument—hoping against hope that he would not.

Despite the fact that Josh put a lot of pressure on Nick to go for the Gold Cup that year, Nick remained adamant that it was the National for Bob and Aldaniti—only the National. It was out of character for him he knew, but even if Aldaniti did not win the race on the day, he would at least have got there and given Bob the chance. His fixation that the two must arrive at Aintree together in one piece was so important that it made the Gold Cup appear totally irrelevant. It simply did not matter. In the end Josh realised how strongly Nick felt and let the matter drop, to Bob's relief. As it turned out it was a far better race than it had appeared on paper and Aldaniti would not have stood a chance of success. Also, he was still sound after the pipe-opener at Ascot and being a very clean winded horse, did not really need another race before the National, unlike other racehorses who need a steady build-up of outings to get them to their peak. Josh, Nick, Bob—all knew that unless there was something wrong with him, Aldaniti put in some of his best performances when he was fresh.

The next problem was keeping him right; arriving at a sensible balance of work that would be neither too demanding nor too relaxing. Josh still rode him each day. He increased the hill work which was good for both Aldaniti's legs and breathing, as well as his general condition. Walking and trotting up the hills, with long, slow canters—always on his own so that he did not start trying to gallop or race—kept Aldaniti going.

Under this steady and controlled regime the legs stayed right, continuing to look cool and tight.

For a horse who enjoyed his work so much, especially the competitive element that came with working in a string, it was not an exciting programme. Before long Aldaniti's usual enthusiasm began to wane. He was less eager, put less effort into his work and looked dangerously close to becoming the sleepy ride that they all knew so well at Barkfold instead of the future National competitor that he was going to be. With another horse it would have been the time for a quick outing to a race to wake him up again. As that was not possible with Aldaniti, Josh came up with another idea that he hoped would freshen him up without causing any over-work or damage.

His friend, Guy Harwood, had an all-weather gallop not too far away that he had said Josh could use if he needed to. Not a person to take advantage of such a generous offer unless it was a real necessity, Josh felt that this would be the answer for Aldaniti. The change of surroundings, the journey, would add together to get the horse's adrenalin running that little bit faster again.

As soon as he saw that Peter Double was putting travelling bandages on his legs instead of the usual exercise bandages, Aldaniti pricked up his ears. That usually meant a trip to the races when he was at Findon. He followed Peter out of his box with more interest than he had shown for some days and almost pulled his lad up the ramp into the horse-box. He may have been disappointed when he was led out to find that he was not at a racecourse, but the journey had given him that bit of edge that Josh had intended. Working in fresh surroundings he put in just enough extra effort without realising what he was doing—exactly as his trainer had hoped; cantering with re-newed enthusiasm, slightly faster than he had been doing in the familiar working areas at Findon, but not so fast that he endangered his legs. He was working more like a racehorse again, which he needed to do if he was to stand a chance of making his journey to Aintree worthwhile, as all the other contenders would have several races to their credit and the extra edge that gives a horse.

As the National grew nearer every day, Aldaniti appeared to be the only one of those involved who remained calm and oblivious to what was going on.

The press, who had already homed in on Bob's remarkable recovery from cancer and then his success that season when twice in three months he had won the Amoco Jockey of the Month award, were showing a great deal of interest in the partnership. Aldaniti's return to fitness after his injuries added to the scope of the stories. One newspaper dubbed the pair "the Crocks of Gold"—which all added pressure to the existing tensions. Nick was so keyed up that he began to have difficulty sleeping. Josh was getting more and more nervous, checking Aldaniti's legs each day, hardly able to let anyone else in the yard do anything for the horse at all. The telephone lines between Kirdford and Findon were almost permanently engaged.

"How are the legs?" Nick would ask as soon as he heard Josh's voice. "Do you think he's going to stay all right? How did he work today?" The questions would fly down the wires, hardly giving Josh time to answer before a new lot were asked: "You *are* still riding him yourself? Are you bandaging him each day? What time are we going to meet at Aintree?"

These calls, mainly for reassurance on Nick's behalf, added to the strain that Josh already felt. It reached the state where neither Nick nor Josh could talk about anything but Aldaniti and his legs, whether they were talking to each other or their wives and families. "He's got to get to Aintree," Nick would say, over and over again.

"We've got to keep him sound," Josh would mutter to himself, or anyone else who would listen. "We've got to."

In the end they were both taking sleeping pills and smoking non-stop as well as driving their wives mad. And Aldaniti's work programme had to go on regardless of the high state of over-excitement that was beginning to take over every day almost before they were awake. There were nine days left to

go. Aldaniti, ridden as usual by Josh, went out with the string
that did road work on Thursdays.

The lanes round Findon are narrow, windy and, in many
places, steep as well. From the Gifford yard it was impossible
to do any serious road work without using the lanes round the
village at some stage of the circuit, and the local traffic had
become used to meeting the strings of horses in the early hours
of the morning. That particular morning, with Josh riding
fourth of the sixteen horses, the leader of the string was
rounding a corner as they were trotting up a hill. He saw a car
flying down the narrow road straight for them. The driver, in
a hurry, late for work, half asleep, panicked and jammed on his
brakes. As the racehorses swung about all over the place,
frightened too, the car skidded, left the road and careered up
the bank. For a moment it looked as if it would turn over and
fall into the horses, then at the last moment the driver was able
to right the car and bring it down to the road without any
further loss of control.

"If it had gone over, Aldaniti would have been one of the
ones who ended up underneath it," Josh said when he was
telling Althea what had happened. He could still see, vividly,
every detail of the car above him on the bank, apparently
going to turn right over and skid through the front half of the
string.

"It didn't, though," Althea said, trying to reassure her
husband, although the thought of the narrow escape that he
had had frightened her too.

Lighting another cigarette Josh could only think how close
it had been, what might have been—"If he hadn't managed
to right it . . ."

"Look," Althea said sensibly, "each day is a day closer.
Aldaniti didn't get hurt . . ." She, in fact, was more concerned
that her husband had escaped injury, although she knew he
was more worried about the horse.

"There's still plenty of time for anything to happen," Josh
said pessimistically. "If it isn't the legs, it could just as well be
something else."

"Nothing's going to go wrong now—we've come this far. It can't. You're doing everything you can to see that the horse is all right. He will be."

"I don't know." Josh shook his head. Knowing how many things could go wrong with any horse, let alone one with dicey legs and so much hope pinned on it, he was not convinced. There was equine 'flu, always a fear at that time of year. Colic. Any number of things.

When Nick rang to check progress that evening, he was as horrified as Josh. "You're sure Aldaniti's all right?" he asked, obviously far more worried about his horse than his friend. "Should I come round and see? I can be there in twenty-five minutes."

"He's fine. No need for you to come round." Josh calmed him down. "We'll just have to keep our fingers crossed from now on—even harder than before."

Other horses in the yard were still racing, and had to be kept going, which helped Josh to keep his feet on the ground while he got over the narrow miss. Much as he would have liked to spend every minute of the day with Aldaniti, he could not. There were forty-nine more horses in the yard, many with problems of their own, which could not be ignored. And Aldaniti was still sound, looking good. With eight days to go, day to day life in the yard had to go on.

At first, when an outbreak of foot and mouth disease was reported on the Isle of Wight, nobody in Sussex took much notice. It was seventy-two hours before Aldaniti was due to start for Liverpool when panic set in after an announcement that Findon was in the area that would be shut off for any movement of livestock if there was another outbreak. Josh had vets and police at the ready to let him know immediately if the zoning became a fact. He lined up temporary stabling further away for Aldaniti and his other Liverpool runners. Then it was a matter of waiting and hoping . . . that if a ban was put on moving horses from the area he would hear about it in time.

The call came on the Wednesday evening—the night before Aldaniti was due to travel—when several of the Gifford horses and their lads were already up at Aintree for the earlier races. There was a possible case near Sompting . . . as soon as it was officially confirmed, that would be it; the area around Findon would be closed off with no movement of any livestock allowed at all.

It was all systems go. While Josh disappeared to find a box, Althea, with the head lad, Ron, and their secretary, Judy—so many of the staff had already gone with the other horses—tore around collecting together anything they could think of that Aldaniti might need for the journey and his stay away. The horse himself was half-way through his evening feed and was surprised to find that he was being rapidly bandaged and prepared for a journey.

He had his first foot on the ramp when a car skidded to a halt beside the horse-box. "It's all right," called out the vet who had phoned through the original warning to Josh. "It was only a scare."

Relieved, but shaky, "I should think it was," Josh declared. "All right, you can bring him down. That was just a dress rehearsal."

The others laughed as Aldaniti was returned to his box and allowed to finish his feed while he was unwrapped and re-settled for the night.

At Barkfold it was a busy Wednesday evening for Valda, who was luckily unaware of the panic going on at Findon. With a horse of her own running in a race on the Thursday of the meeting, she and Nick were leaving early the following morning, staying away until the Saturday evening. Her son, Alastair, would be driving the rest of the family up on Friday afternoon—Euan, Nicholas and the very excited thirteen-year-old Alexandra. With Nick in such a state of panic that he was no help at all, Valda had to make sure that all the arrangements were made, that they had enough clothes for the two nights they would be away, that there was enough food for the children until they came up, and that the other horses were also all right and everyone knew what was going on, where and when.

It was an apprehensive couple who got into the car the next morning. Nick was uptight, Valda tense, too. All the staff turned out to see them off and send their "good lucks" to Aldaniti. At last they were off, waving, down the drive and out of sight of the house. Nick did not have much to talk about apart from Aldaniti, but that topic of conversation kept him going for the whole journey without any trouble at all and left Valda time to unwind. As long as she put in the occasional "yes", "mm" and "no", Nick thought she was listening and was happy.

They met Josh in the parade ring where Valda's Stonepark was getting ready for his run in the Topham Trophy. Nick quickly checked that Aldaniti had left Findon on schedule —still sound!—before lighting another cigarette so that he could concentrate on the racing.

Stonepark was another horse who had been off with leg trouble, had come back into form well and was starting among the favourites for his race. His jockey was Richard Rowe, who could manage the lighter weight of ten stone that was all that was needed for the race and would have been virtually impossible for Bob to make.

The nine-year-old Stonepark had won several races that season and looked all set for another success to get the meeting off to a good start for the Embiricoses and Josh. The first fence of the Topham is one of the smaller National fences, about four foot seven inches. Stonepark took off keenly, but over-jumped, falling badly, so seriously hurt that he had to be destroyed. Disaster striking so early in the meeting was a blow to them all.

Valda was heartbroken. All her horses meant so much to her, especially the brave ones like Stonepark who came back as keen after an injury as before. The inevitable rare tragedies that went with National Hunt racing always hurt her badly. Nick, as well, was terribly upset, both for his wife and her horse. Although he had learned early on that the challenge of jump racing could not be met without accidents happening, he, too, still found them hard to accept when they did occur. With Valda so deeply upset it was doubly painful.

The death of Stonepark naturally brought back to both Nick and Valda the loss of their cousins' horse Alverton in the National itself two years earlier. Nick, superstitious at the best of times, could not help thinking briefly—would Aldaniti make it three? Accidents were said to come three at a time. In a moment of black despair the thought flashed through his mind that perhaps he should not run the risk—pull Aldaniti out before anything happened to him.

Josh was another person who could never take the racing tragedies lightly. He also realised what it would mean to Nick . . . and then he relaxed; to enjoy racing, you had to be able to take the rough with the smooth—and Nick knew that as well as anyone.

Nick's indecision had been momentary. Aldaniti would run. They had not come through to get so close with the horse—on top of which was all that Bob had been through too; they had to go on and have a go at it for the sake of everybody who cared. Later, when he was alone with Valda and they were able to talk quietly about the loss of her horse she, too, was adamant that Aldaniti must run as planned. However upset she was herself they could not disappoint the thousands of people who were pinning their hopes on Bob's chances—amazed that he had come so far after being so terribly ill—seeing the next step he was to take as a message of hope. The whole matter of Bob, Aldaniti and the National had become a dream to so many people. It could not be shattered at that stage.

Nick and Valda stayed on at the meeting as Aldaniti was due to arrive after the long, slow journey from Findon. They went through to the stables to see their horse who appeared none the worse for his nine-hour journey and had settled into his new box with the help of Peter Double. With clean water and good hay there if he wanted them, Aldaniti was happily surveying his new surroundings, watching the comings and goings in the busy yard, well aware that he was at last back at a race-course.

"He's fine," Valda said.

"Did he travel well?" Nick asked Peter.

"Super," Peter assured him. "Slept most of the way we reckon."

Nick patted his horse. "Well, you've got this far . . ." he wondered; who could not help but wonder—especially when there were another forty-eight hours to go before they would know the answer. "Come on," he said to Valda. He was finding it difficult to concentrate and pass the time. "Let's go and watch the last race. I think Bob's got a ride in it."

From the stands they were horrified to see their jockey take a crashing fall and remain lying on the ground while one of the back-runners trampled over him. "Oh no!" Nick could not believe it. What more could go wrong?

"That looked nasty," Valda cried, as they waited impatiently to see if Bob would get up of his own accord.

"He's up," Nick said with a sigh of relief, "but he doesn't look so good," he added, as he saw Bob limp to the side, hunched up, obviously hurt and in pain. "It can't be serious," Nick said hopefully. "I just don't believe it."

"We'd better go down and see," Valda said and started down from their viewpoint on top of the stand. With Nick behind her, horrified at the thought that although Aldaniti was all right it now looked as if Bob might be out of it, she managed to find a way through the crowds who were beginning to make their way home for the day. Nick followed. He thought he had come to terms with the ups and downs of racing years ago. This he could not take in. "If he's too bad . . ." he said, knowing how tough the course doctors are with jockeys after a fall.

Bob was indeed in a lot of pain. When he got to the changing room he told the doctor that he had not hurt himself at all—anything rather than miss the ride on Aldaniti that meant so much. Like most jockeys Bob had had back trouble for a long time. It's inevitable with all the falls they take. It was his back that hurt then—badly. Later, when he was changing, he found the vivid imprint of a horse-shoe, bright red, stamped on his back. With Aldaniti very lucky to have got off with a good weight from the handicapper, ten stone thirteen pounds, instead of well over eleven as they had expected, Bob still had to watch his weight. The couple of hours that he spent in the sauna that evening helped his back as well.

With a lot of their friends up in Liverpool for the meeting, the Embiricoses joined a group for dinner. Bob could not eat much. He also had to hide from Josh how much his back was hurting him—not easy when the trainer knew he had had a fall and would be trying to conceal anything really serious. He managed to put up a good enough show to convince them all that he was a lot better than he really felt.

When Nick woke on the Friday morning he began to remember a dream he had had. It was still vividly clear in his mind . . . Aldaniti had won the National . . . there were so many people . . . he had been desperately trying to get through the crowds . . . the mud . . . battling and fighting to get to his horse . . . only to wake just before he reached him. Not usually a person who could recall his dreams so clearly, Nick did not tell Valda about it—or Josh and Althea—in case it brought bad luck, which was the last thing they needed any more of after the previous day.

But Valda was obviously more cheerful that morning, which encouraged Nick. When they were told by Josh that Bob had ridden Aldaniti out early in the morning and reported him as being fine—"no problems from the journey: pulling like a train"—the gloom left over from the day before cleared completely. With no horses of their own running that day, Nick and Valda remained reasonably relaxed, bumping into friends and generally enjoying a day at the races without the worry and strain that they felt when they were there as owners. Expectations for the following day were brought up all around them, and Nick was able to say quite confidently that Aldaniti had travelled well, was eating well—and was still sound.

Bob spent Friday morning in the sauna, after his ride on Aldaniti, as his back had stiffened considerably during the night. He had one ride that afternoon in a novice hurdle, which he finished without a place and only minor trouble from the bruise. It had been the test he needed, though, to see how much of a problem the bruise was going to be. At least he had made it—one step nearer to the promise he had made in the papers a week before when he had claimed: "I'll win it . . . for everyone who's helped me . . . and most of all the patients still in hospital . . ."

Alastair, Nicholas, Euan and Alexandra arrived at their parents' hotel fairly early that evening.

"Did you have a good drive up?" Valda asked them.

Alexandra brushed that aside. "How is he?"

"Who?" her mother asked, puzzled.

"Aldaniti, of course," Alexandra said impatiently.

Very like her father in many ways, Alexandra was almost as teed up as he was. Bob's recovery had meant a lot to her, as had Aldaniti's. The two tackling the National together was as important to her as it was to her father. Since January she too had been dreaming about the race. Her first dream had seen the pair fall at Becher's. The next time she had dreamt the impossible—that Aldaniti had been beaten by a mare. Then, at last, she had dreamt that the pair had won.

"He's fine," Nick told her. "Settled in and looking forward to tomorrow."

"Bob's being interviewed on television in a minute," Valda reminded her family. "Find the programme, Alastair. We mustn't miss that."

Red Rum was also on television that evening being asked who he thought was going to win the National. His handler put his ear to Red Rum's mouth and listened before turning to the camera. "He said Aldaniti!" he reported, to cheers of delight from the family.

Eleven of them set out for dinner that evening at an Italian Restaurant in Southport—Nick and Valda and their children, Josh and Althea and their son Nicholas, and Bob and his girlfriend Jo Beswick. There was one topic of conversation throughout the evening that everyone returned to again and again. More friends joined them until the party numbered twenty, among them Monty Court who kept them all laughing with a stream of stories. But instead of the high state of nervous tension that might have been expected it turned into a noisy but strangely confident evening. Bob was the only one who could not enjoy the food and drink, and was perhaps the quietest member of the party.

There seemed to be almost two different levels of vibrations in the air. On one hand there was a sense of disbelief that they were all actually there together the night before the National. The fact that Bob had recovered, and Aldaniti too, made it too much of a fairy tale—they would never win the race. And on the other hand a lot of them were so calm it was almost as if they had won already.

With a general feeling that to lose the next day was completely out of the question, the party made its way back to the hotel bar—where other owners and trainers had the same feeling about their own horses. Nick was soon in conversation with a hearty Irishman who was convinced that his horse would out-run Aldaniti.

"If we win I'll buy you a glass of champagne," Nick offered.

"I'll be buying you one," the Irishman said confidently.

Bob and Aldaniti were the only two gentlemen to wake up completely clear-headed on the Saturday morning. By the time Nick and Valda woke at 6 a.m., their horse was already putting away a light breakfast of oats and nuts while Peter Double had a cup of tea before returning to the box to muck out and tack him up, ready for the traditional early morning ride.

After a glass of champagne while they were waiting for the whole party to appear downstairs, they were off—Nick travelling with Josh and Althea, Euan with Valda, Alexandra and Nicholas following behind with Alastair at the wheel of their car.

"We're going to have to stop for petrol," Alastair warned the others.

"There's a garage," Nicholas pointed out.

Let loose for the first time after winning the Grand National,
Aldaniti uses up some of his energy

Above: Aldaniti in retirement with his owner, Nick Embiricos

Below: Aldaniti meets another National winner, Kilmore

"Do hurry up," urged Alexandra who did not want to miss a moment of the day on the racecourse.

While the attendant was filling the car he put his head into the window. "You got a horse in the National then?" he asked, as not many locals were about that early. The Liverpudlians had only just gone to bed.

"Yes. Aldaniti," Alexandra told him excitedly.

"I'll have to put a bet on him," the man said, "it must be a lucky omen your pulling in here."

"Good luck," the family called.

"And to you," the man waved after them.

When the Giffords arrived in the car park on time, Althea was so used to their being late everywhere they went that she did not like it: "Something is bound to go wrong now," she said gloomily. "We're never on time for anything."

It was a thoroughly relaxed group who walked out on to the course first thing that Saturday to join the few other trainers and owners who were also due to watch their horses work. Peter was ready with Aldaniti. He trotted the horse quietly round the almost empty car park to loosen up while his jockey and connections watched appreciatively. Aldaniti really did look better than any of them had seen him before. Then Peter was sliding off, and Josh legged Bob into the saddle.

"He's looking super," Nick said, almost as if he could not believe that this was really happening.

"Fantastic!" agreed Alexandra, still as fond of the horse as she had ever been.

Valda, who was still worried that the legs would not stand up to the long four-mile race, agreed with her husband. "He's never looked better."

"Canter him down a bit, Bob," Josh suggested, "just to give him a bit of a stretch and get him used to the place."

Bob turned the big chestnut round and cantered him quietly away from the group. The early morning sunlight glinted on his highly polished coat as the powerful muscles moved beneath the skin. Bob turned him back, cantered past and pulled him up.

"He's spot on," he said with a grin. "Better than he's ever been!"

Josh patted the horse that so many people had such high hopes for. "Take him out for a pick of grass, Peter," he said, "then put him away."

People were beginning to trickle into the car parks and on to the grounds, to mingle with the remnants of litter—torn up betting slips and tossed away cigarette packets left over from the previous two days' racing—missed by the overnight clearance team.

It was several years since Nick had last visited Aintree, and as they started out to walk the course and plan the best route for Bob to take with Aldaniti he felt very strange. To him the day had a magical sparkle to it, a special air that he could not quite explain. In one way he felt that the win was going to be on—despite it being too much of a fairy tale to be possible. Yet it could not be possible . . . The National was such a lottery. The first ever horse to win the race had been called that —Lottery. Bob was better, Aldaniti was better, they could not really ask for any more. Yet he was equally sure that it was going to happen—that matters were well beyond his control, in the hands of Someone who already knew the outcome.

The worst fear that any of them had, except for the legs not standing up to it, was that Aldaniti might start in his usual bold, extravagant way and overjump. Bob felt sure that if he could hold him together over the first few fences he would realise that these were bigger than anything he had seen before and not be quite so reckless.

Josh, who had ridden in the National many times during his own very successful racing career, coming in second in 1967, was a believer in the theory of keeping to the outside of the course. The jumps are a little bit lower, and although you have further to travel, he believed that riding the outside, Bob would stand a better chance of getting round.

"There's so much chance to the National," Valda remarked as they were walking round. "One horse down, and a dozen more can come down with it."

"I must say, I'd forgotten how really big these fences are," Nick said, extremely glad that he preferred being an owner to a jockey. "They're completely different to anything on a normal course."

Valda nodded. "They're vast," she agreed.

Alexandra was also impressed by the size of the fences. As she looked at the third fence, with the first ditch of the course, she drew a mental comparison between it and the fences that she asked her pony to jump when they were competing in Junior Pony Club events.

"That is pretty horrific," she declared, but in no way put off. For her Aintree and the Grand National was also becoming a dream. A different one from her father's, admittedly, although she did not even know about his. Alexandra did not want to own the winner necessarily, unless she happened to be able to jockey it as well. That day she began to want to ride the winner of the National when she was older. She still felt the same when she stood underneath Becher's Brook which towered above her from the landing side. The thought of actually riding that drop was something to look forward to—not be afraid of. With the right horse, and more experience on her part, it should be possible.

The ground on the middle to inside of the course had become terribly cut up after the Canal Turn, fence number eight, which had been used in the previous days' racing. So again it was decided that Bob must ride wide, there especially, where the going was so much better on the outside and much less likely to tire Aldaniti or put extra strain on his legs.

The ditch at the Chair is on the take-off side, six foot wide. Alexandra lay down in it, with her hands above her head. "What are those little gates for?" she asked.

"Taking out the horses that fall," one of her brothers told her cheerfully. "Did you know that this ditch is wide enough to drive a Land Rover through?"

Alexandra had not known, and was suitably impressed. It was with a slight feeling of envy that she waved goodbye to Bob at the end of their walk round one complete circuit of the course—the horses that stayed up had to go round twice.

For Bob it was time for another visit to the sauna where most of his friends would be passing the morning. All of them nervous, waiting, passing the time. The quiet ones talking nineteen to the dozen—the talkative ones locked into an anxious silence. The Giffords and Embiricoses returned to their hotel for their breakfast. Several glasses of champagne later, when they had changed, paid their bills, and were returning to the course, Nick saw the picture of Red Rum in the hall. He touched it quickly. "Wish us luck," he said quietly.

CHAPTER SIX

What a horse!

Once again arriving on time at the course, Althea was convinced that things were still going too smoothly. "There's no panic, we're not late. It's almost uncanny," she said.

"There's nothing more we can do anyhow," Josh said. "Apart from see them off. It's up to Bob and Aldaniti now."

Some of them had lunch. Nick was too uptight. Then the horses were being led out for the big race. Aldaniti had been plaited, rugged up, and finally prepared for the parade ring some time ago, but despite the biggest crowd he had ever seen, he walked beside Peter Double as quietly as usual, with that little bit of extra life he always showed when he knew that he was going to race.

Althea, who was with her ten-year-old son Nicholas, wanted to join Josh, Nick and Valda and their family and Bob's girlfriend, Jo Beswick, in the paddock. Children as young as Nicholas were not allowed in. Looking at the milling, excited crowds, she did not know what to do. It was hardly the ideal place to leave a child alone.

"Wait here—exactly here. I'll come out once they leave the paddock and we'll go up to the stand together," she said eventually, unable to think of anything else that she could do.

"O.K."

"You're not to go off," she insisted.

"No. I won't," Nicholas said.

Bob had already weighed out, exactly right, which allowed him to ride in his favourite 3 lb. saddle—one he found much more comfortable than the even lighter ones. Last minute instructions were coming from Josh.

"You know what to do, Bob. Keep out of trouble the first time round. Just hunt round. Then you can think about winning," he reminded the jockey, who was still looking remarkably calm, despite so many outside pressures on top of the ones shared by the other jockeys. "The best of luck," he added as he legged Bob on to Aldaniti.

"Good luck, Bob," from Nick and Valda, and Althea and Jo.

Then he was led away by Peter for another lap of the crowded parade ring, before leaving to parade in front of the stands and then canter down to the start.

The rest of the party had agreed to watch the race together on top of the stands. The meeting place had been arranged earlier. Althea's first concern was her son Nicholas. Pushing and struggling through the crowds she got back at last to the spot where she had left him. He was not there—nowhere to be seen. It was hopeless looking for a small boy in those crowds, but for a moment or two she did. Then, as he was a very independent child, and Althea was desperate to get up to Josh or she knew that she would never see anything of the race, she decided to leave him to it and head for the others. She was a little bit worried as she again fought the crowds to get up to the top of the stand, but he had been up there with them earlier and knew where they intended to watch the race from. Perhaps he would be there already?

"Have you seen Nicholas?" she asked Josh when she finally squeezed in beside him.

"No." But at that stage Josh was too worried about Bob and Aldaniti to really take in that their son was missing in the massive, seething crowds around and below them.

The rest of the party felt a mixture of varying emotions. Valda, still not confident that Aldaniti could stand the race, looked up at the sky as if to say, "We've done all we can, it's over to You now." Valda usually shut her eyes or turned away at each fence when a 'chase was in progress, and her feelings that day had reached the state where she did not really want to watch any of the National at all.

Nick, on the other hand, was strangely relaxed—more so than he could remember. For once his hands did not shake as he watched the horses collecting at the start. Nor was he impatient at the inevitable delay. With his elbows resting on Alexandra's shoulders, he could hold his binoculars still without any trouble. Josh was the one shaking so much that he could hardly see through his at all, and Althea picked up her husband's tension.

The thirty-nine runners for the 1981 Sun Grand National were eventually off. Aldaniti, well on the outside as he was meant to be, tried to overjump the first as they had feared, but managed to pull himself together and gallop on to the second.

"Where is he Josh?" Nick asked, trying to find his horse in the usual chaos of the first few fences. "Is he all right?" he persisted—totally unaware that Josh was beyond knowing where the horse was—to him it was all a blur.

"There he is!" shouted Alexandra, when Aldaniti jumped his way into the lead after the twelfth. From then it was obvious where Aldaniti was—his big white blaze standing out as boldly as Nick's colours—and Josh was able to follow the rest of the race.

"He's gone to the front too soon," Nick cried in horror. "He'll never keep the lead from there!"

"He's going fine. Jumping super!" Josh said. But like Nick he was worried that they had gone out in front too soon. The plan to hunt round the first circuit had obviously been beyond Bob's powers of persuasion.

"He's jumped his way past the others!"

"But he can't go on alone." Nick was dreadfully worried.

"He stays all day," Josh reminded him, his binoculars firmly glued to the distinctive white blaze.

Bob was equally surprised to find himself out in front so soon, although Aldaniti had simply gained ground each time he flew a fence. He knew, though, that if he got beaten after that he would be in real trouble from Josh for not following the plan they had worked out. There was nothing he could do but keep going. Aldaniti still had not settled—even in front he was shaking his head against Bob's restraining hands, pulling like a train, wanting to go even faster.

As Aldaniti headed for the Chair, with Zongalero, Royal Stuart and Rubstic—all good horses—not far behind him, Nick held his breath. Valda could not look at all. "Tell me how he does it," she asked as she turned away.

The horse saw a stride, ears pricked, stood well off, to a groan from Nick, and then made it look absolutely nothing. "He's O.K.," Nick told Valda.

"I think he's running away with Bob," Josh shouted.

By then the noise of the crowd had increased to show that they too realised who was out in front. Not many of them were unaware of Bob's remarkable recovery, and how much he had done already to give encouragement to other people who were ill.

Aldaniti flew each fence, jumping them with even greater style and enthusiasm than any one of them had imagined he was capable of. Obviously enjoying every minute of the race, with ears pricked, he was eating up the fences, making them look easy, instead of the formidable obstacles they really were. He took off for the seventeenth fence stride for stride with Rubstic, to land four lengths ahead. Becher's saw Aldaniti on the inside, jumping breathtakingly. There was a gasp from the crowd as he pitched on landing—and a sigh of relief as Bob picked him up and kept him going, still well clear of the others.

The Canal Turn was coming up. Bob wanted to take it at an

angle and asked Aldaniti to stand well off. The horse responded. And again stood off at the next, galloping well, strong and powerful. "What a horse!" thought Bob as he tried to give him a breather in between the fences. "He's out of this world."

With three fences to go, Bob and Aldaniti were still well out on their own. Bob knew that Aldaniti had too much heart to give up, however tired he was. He also knew that the more tired Aldaniti became, the more danger there was of him damaging that leg. Royal Mail was still in touch two lengths behind. Ten lengths behind were three others, including Aldaniti's greatest rival Spartan Missile, who was making ground after an earlier mistake.

The crowd were spellbound. Would these two make it? Bob, who had been so ill, and the horse who had also suffered?

On top of the stands Josh was wondering just how much Aldaniti had taken out of himself by the long run out in front. With the slight preparation they had given him, did the horse really have the endurance to hold his own on the long run in, so long that many a good horse had been beaten there? With two fences to go, and that dreaded tiring run in still in front of them, Bob and Aldaniti were still out in front.

"He'll never do it!" Nick said, beginning to feel that he was somewhere above himself, watching his body watch the race without him. It was all totally unreal.

Coming up behind the pair that the crowd was screaming for, and willing to win, on the long run in, gaining steadily, was John Thorne on Spartan Missile. For a moment it looked as if he might make it. Then near the finish it was obvious that Spartan Missile was too tired . . . Bob waved his stick in the air, his face one big grin, as he and Aldaniti passed the post—to win.

John Thorne, coming in second, who would have dearly loved to win the race as much as anyone, was the first to congratulate his friend as soon as they had steadied their tired horses, giving Bob a hearty clap on the back.

Feeling as if it was not him at all, tears of delight and wonder streaming down his face, Nick joined the excited crowd who were all heading for the winner—his horse. Exactly like the dream he had two nights before, he had to fight and push and struggle to get through. When he finally reached Aldaniti, the horse was being led in on one side by a large man whose equally large friend helped try to keep Nick away.

"Get out of the way," Nick said through the tears as he tried to grab the bridle. "It's my horse." Peter Double had hold of the other side of the bridle.

At last he had him. Collar and tie askew, tie-pin lost forever, hair all over the place. "Well done, Bob!" Nick patted the horse whose tongue hung out with tiredness while Bob grinned, unable to take it all in either. "Fantastic."

Valda had also managed to get through the crowds and grabbed hold of Aldaniti's tail so that she would not get separated from him again. The roars of the crowd were as great as those in 1977 when Red Rum had completed his hat-trick.

In the winner's enclosure they were all in tears—Josh, Althea, Nick, Valda. Many people in the crowd were crying, too, aware that they had just watched one of the most emotional wins that racing had ever seen. Bob Champion, the jockey who had been so ill that no one had thought he would ever ride again, and Aldaniti the horse who really should not have been able to stand such an endurance test at all. The pair had caught the emotions of the crowd before the race—now their achievement caused pandemonium at Aintree. Aldaniti was tired, that was obvious as he stood breathing heavily, drenched in sweat, nostrils flared, head not as high as usual. He knew, though, that all those people were cheering for just one horse—himself. Bright-eyed, ears pricked, he took it all in as Peter Double and the head travelling lad, Snowy Davis, removed Bob's saddle and threw a sweat rug over his steaming back.

Then Alexandra appeared. Lost in the crowds, thinking she would never get through, her father's friend Henry Pelham had grabbed a policeman. "She's the owner's daughter," he had explained urgently. "Can you get her through to the winner's enclosure?" By the time her escort had got her through the crowds Alexandra was in floods of tears like the rest of her family. Young Nicholas Gifford also appeared in the winner's enclosure—to his mother's relief. Quite by chance in those massive crowds he had been spotted by his Godfather who had taken him to Aldaniti and his parents. One by one Alexandra's brothers found their way to Aldaniti as well, to one of the most emotional family scenes they could remember.

For a horse who had just galloped four-and-a-half miles, most of them out on his own, with thirty fences to take, Aldaniti put up with the hugs and affectionate pats that came from all directions very calmly. It was his day, after all. Tired as he was, he loved every minute of it.

Back at Kirdford, where Beryl had thirty people squashed into her living room to watch the race on television, the atmosphere was equally emotional. Many in tears, unable to believe that it had really happened after all. Wilf was not with them, though. Convinced that Aldaniti would never stand up to the race with his leg problems, he had gone to the local point-to-point for the afternoon. But the cheers of those who had been watching on television in the Stable bungalow were as proud and excited as any at Aintree.

Eventually it was time for the triumphant horse to be led away and made comfortable after his efforts. He would be washed off, scraped dry, and then allowed to relax. For Bob, Nick and Josh there were the inevitable television interviews. When Bob was eventually grabbed, the main subject was his own incredible achievement. He was shy . . . disbelieving. "Don't forget the trainer," he insisted. "It was a great piece of training to bring Aldaniti back to win the National after three bad injuries and only one run in eighteen months."

When he did speak about his own illness he explained: "I rode this race for all the patients still in hospital. And for all the people who look after them. My only wish is that my winning shows them that there is always hope, and all battles can be won."

For Nick, who had the same strong feeling, that was almost too much. It was time to receive the large porcelain Grand National Trophy and he was still shaking like a leaf. "Could you hold on to your side as well? I'm afraid I'm going to drop it," he said to Lady Lamb who was making the presentation on behalf of the race sponsors, *The Sun* newspaper.

The first chance to relax had arrived. Valda, Althea, Jo and their children were shown into the comparative peace of *The Sun* newspaper's box. Alexandra sat down on the nearest chair, still with tears streaming down her face.

"Is something the matter?" a young man asked with genuine concern. "Why are you crying so much?"

"We've just won the National—we're so happy," Alexandra tried to explain.

Meanwhile Josh, Nick and Bob had been guided away by the Assistant Clerk of the Course. "There's a little room round here where you can have a quiet glass of champagne," he said.

"Sounds great," agreed Nick, still extremely overwrought, as was Josh. Bob looked as if he had still not come down to earth either.

Expecting peace, a chance to try and say the hundred and one things they wanted to say to each other, they were surprised to find around sixty members of the press waiting for them. The champagne was there. Nick could hardly hold his glass.

"We must be sensible," Josh insisted. "We've got the drive back—we want to make it in time to watch the re-run on television."

"Cheers!" Nick agreed, as they prepared to face a further barrage of questions—at least they had something to help fortify them that time.

Still unable to take in what had happened, the rest of the day was a haze for the Embiricoses as they talked through the race again and again. For Josh and Bob there was another horse and another race before they could think of going home, as well as a constant supply of champagne.

Nick and Valda went through to the stables to see how

Aldaniti was. Washed down and comfortable again Peter had him out picking grass.

"He looks as if winning the National is something you do every day," Nick laughed.

"He would," said a delighted Peter. "He's fine—no bumps that I can see and the legs feel tight and cool."

"I wonder if they will tomorrow," Valda thought as they gave the horse a final pat of congratulations before leaving him to relax.

At last it was time to begin the journey home. The convoy of cars set out together with Nick and Josh inseparable as well as the worse for wear. Althea drove her car with the two men asleep in the back on either side of Nicholas. Valda and Euan followed her. Behind them came the rest of the family. They stopped for a non-alcoholic meal—all they could get at a Motorway service station—and then continued their journey to their friend, Tim Fox, where they stopped to watch the evening re-play of the National.

Josh and Althea then had to go on to Findon. It was already very late. They were amazed to find the pub, the Village House, still open—in fact waiting up for them in the hope that they would drop in. Yet more celebrations, before they could at last get home and pile into bed around 3 a.m.

The Embiricoses arrived home eventually as well, with the trophy to be unwrapped and admired—as tangible proof for Nick that he had not been dreaming all day. Aldaniti and Bob had won the National. The porcelain trophy—blue, gold and white with a scene from a past National painted on the front—was theirs to keep for ever, as were the six individually painted matching plates picturing varying scenes each year.

"Here's to Aldaniti," Nick said as he poured champagne all round.

"Cheers!" The family touched glasses and toasted their hero.

"And Bob," Alexandra added.

"And Bob," the voices echoed.

Bob was, in fact, back home in Wiltshire, after dinner with

his rival John Thorne, while his health was being drunk at Barkfold. He had had to stop and buy an evening paper before he finally believed that he had at last reached the goal that had kept him going when he was at his worst—of winning the Grand National on Aldaniti. "I was just a passenger on him really," he said to his friend Jonathan Powell who was with him. "He did it all after the first two."

They all knew that there would be a reception party for Aldaniti when he returned to Findon on the Sunday. It's traditional with any National or Derby winner. Josh had expected the usual two or three hundred people, mainly locals, to be the most that they would have to cope with. So he and Althea were quite unprepared when the first phone call came through to them at 7.30 a.m. asking what time they were expecting Aldaniti. Althea then had a constant flow of calls, all asking the same question, which made it impossible for her to get dressed. Most of them were from complete strangers, calling from all over the country. The telephone just rang and rang. Eventually her daughter Tina had to take over so that Althea did not have to go out to meet Aldaniti in her night-clothes.

Tina had not been to Liverpool with them as she did not like travelling very much. As she began to realise what fun they must have had she wished that she had been with them. Nicholas' remarks and stories about his adventures—coming in between telephone calls—made Tina feel a bit left out. But as the people began to arrive there was so much to do, and at last she was right in the middle of it all, that there was no more time for regrets. It was simply a matter of helping her mother and enjoying herself.

Bob, who had driven up from Wiltshire, was amazed to find the narrow streets of Findon overflowing with people. More than three thousand well-wishers turned out to see Aldaniti arrive, bringing home to all the horse's connections exactly how much the win had meant.

Nick and Valda and their family were amazed too. "I never expected anything like this!" Nick, still up in the clouds with delight, was soon greeting Josh and Bob, slapping them on the back before talking through the race. They did not have long to wait. Snowy Davis had agreed to stop the horse-box and ring the Giffords when he was about ten minutes away.

"Change his travelling gear," Josh said. "Put on his sash, and the winner's sheet. Oh, and put a bridle on him. You'll have to unload him in the village—you'll never get the horse-box through."

Perhaps the least surprised of them all at this reception, Aldaniti arrived home to Findon and treated the crowds as if there were that many people all over the village every day. Tired, but still wound up from the race so that he was wide awake and alert, Aldaniti behaved exactly as if he had been rehearsed for this welcome—and as if it was his due. He knew that all those people had come to see him, to pat him and touch him and stroke him. As he walked quietly through the crowded streets his natural presence caught the eye and his own excited state added to the already highly emotional state of many of his well-wishers.

With another horse there might well have been an accident. People patted him and touched him where they liked and at will as Peter Double led the hero home. Aldaniti accepted it all. It was obvious from his bouncy walk, the way he continually bit his tongue, and his air of enjoyment that he loved being the focus of attention and was going to make the best of every minute of it. Climbing the hill from the village to the Gifford yard he played to his audience gently but surely. The photo sessions, the popping of yet more champagne corks, the whirring of the television cameras, the flash-lights, the "oohs" and "aahs", were all accepted naturally by this amazing horse that just the day before had actually been enjoying tackling the most hair-raising fences in National Hunt racing—and now behaved as calmly as a police-horse.

All sorts of flags, blue and white for Nick's colours, the Union Jack for Josh, were flapping in the wind above his stable door. There were cards from the stable lads and the visitors; telegrams of congratulations as well, including one signed by the four grandchildren of his breeder, Tommy Barron, after whom Aldaniti had been named—Alastair and David Cook, and Nicola and Timothy Barron. Ribbons and bows, too. At last he was put in his box. The smart new sheet came off to be replaced by a warmer jute rug. The leg bandages were removed. The bridle was taken off. Left alone with water, hay and a sackful of carrots in his manger Aldaniti watched the continuing chaos in the yard between mouthfuls. It was not every day that Josh lost all his daffodils under trampling feet, or that the police had to be called in to help control the traffic in the yard. Aldaniti did not intend to miss a minute of this strange variation in the usually tidy, well-regulated yard.

As the celebrations continued without Aldaniti, Beryl found her husband. "His legs are fine!" she said, astounded. "It was the first thing I did as soon as I got a chance. Check them over. There's no heat—they're tighter than ever."

Gradually the visitors began to drift away. They had had their reasons for travelling to Findon that day. Some were purely locals who wanted to support "their" horse. Others had come out of curiosity after reading about the amazing win in the Sunday papers. The most important, though, came through their understanding of exactly what the victory that Bob and Aldaniti had achieved between them really meant —that there were times when it was possible to beat the odds if you really put your mind to it—crises could be overcome, life need never be completely black.

Late in the afternoon the Giffords and the Embiricoses managed to get away for lunch together in the pub at Findon, The Village House. Again the talk was of the race the day before, fence by fence, stride by stride, until they began to feel that they knew it off by heart.

"We must have a party for everyone who's been involved with the horse," Nick decided.

"Oh yes," Alexandra was as keen as her brothers. "Let's have it here."

"Would that be possible?" Nick asked.

"I'll go and check," Josh said. He was only away a few

minutes. "That'll be fine. If we can let them know roughly how many as soon as possible," he added.

They started planning it there and then. All the lads from the Gifford yard to start with, plus their girlfriends. The staff from Barkfold, vets, blacksmiths, horse-box drivers, everyone who had been involved with Aldaniti. Getting in touch with some of them was going to mean hours on the telephone. As they were all tired anyway, the Embiricoses made their way home to go on with the arrangements from there.

Nick was still overwrought. He knew that while to win the Gold Cup at Cheltenham was the ambition of many people, as it is the staying champion 'chase where all the horses compete at level weights so the best one wins, the National is a handicap 'chase and it is the best horse on the day—plus a lot of luck—that wins it; this had been his secret dream since March 1965 when his great friend Tommy Smith came over from America and rode to win the National on Jay Trump trained by Fred Winter. On top of this had been Bob Champion's need of something to look forward to to keep him going and he had latched on to Aldaniti and the National. Then Aldaniti had broken down . . . it had all looked impossible. But it had happened in the end, and Nick could think no further ahead than that he needed a day off from work. The office would not be seeing him on the Monday morning; it had all become too much emotionally.

It was a sensible decision to have made. Apart from arranging the party for that evening, Valda would have been swamped under the letters and telegrams that had the postman staggering the next day—and for several days to come. Many people phoned. Some friends, mostly strangers. The Embiricoses were once again overwhelmed by the genuine response their horse's win had brought from everybody. Each letter was answered, not personally signed by the horse himself, but inside a photograph of Aldaniti with Bob, signed by Nick. No one person could have coped with it all on their own. Even with Valda's help both he and she found it extremely hard work.

The party at Findon was Nick's way of saying "thank you" to all the people who had helped to make his dream come true. Josh and Althea, who felt that all the horses in the yard were "theirs" were as thrilled and grateful as Nick and Valda. Still tired, and with the lads knowing that they would have to be out in the yard at 6 a.m. as usual or they would have the Governor after them, everyone was so happy, the sense of achievement so high, that that party at The Village House will always be remembered by the people lucky enough to have been part of it.

The gradual process of letting down began for Aldaniti. As Peter Double took him out alone around the streets of Findon many of the locals would stop him. "Is that the horse that won the National?" they asked. When Peter said that it was, Aldaniti was patted, made much of and stuffed with the peppermints he loved. Before long the villagers recognised him as he came through each day—and Aldaniti recognised the ones that wanted to chat and pass the time of day, quite happy to stop for them as they made a fuss of him.

Within a month of the race Aldaniti was loaded into the horse-box to make the return journey to Barkfold Manor. On the way there was a short delay while he was guest of honour at the Kirdford village fête. Then he was home, in his own yard. His welcome that time was the best he had ever had. Beryl, Wilf, Lin Wilcox and Margaret Phillips were all there to see him home, relieved that he was sound, proud of his success. Still too fit to be turned out, he was gradually let down and roughed off.

In most ways he was the same old Aldaniti—slightly sleepy, hacking round the lanes, well mannered in and out of the stable. To Beryl, though, he was a greater responsibility than he had ever been. When the weather was right and it was time to turn him out she was afraid that he would explode as usual and damage his legs. It was decided that the best thing to do, and the safest, would be to turn him out in the all-weather school, especially designed to give a soft, stress-free area for working horses whatever the weather, with little chance of

ven Aldaniti coming to harm whatever he did. Fenced all
ound to stop escape, with a deep bed of shavings, it was the
deal place to let him get rid of any high spirits that he had.

So the next June afternoon, with the sun warm and inviting,
Aldaniti had his legs bandaged and was led out to the school,
ll three girls going to watch. Set loose, with the gate shut
ehind him, Aldaniti did not realise immediately what was
oing on. He stood in the sunshine head up, eyes bright,
waiting. Then he was off. Galloping round in the shavings,
squealing with delight at being free. His hind legs kicked out
igh behind him, his tail swishing with the sheer pleasure of
ife. Round and round he went, releasing all the pent up
motions that had built up through the long period in training
nd the National itself.

Skidding to a halt beside the fence, he called out his return.
Horses in the surrounding fields answered. Aldaniti swung
ound into a frenzied gallop, bucking and twisting, before
topping and squealing again. He was answered as the other
horses picked up his excitement and also began to charge about
heir fields. Then he went down to roll, over and over and
over, his mouth wide open with exhilaration. Up and down,
up and down. At last he stood, spread his legs and shook
himself, sending showers of shavings in all directions. With
shavings stuck in his mane and tail he trotted proudly round
he school. He was back, he called to his friends in the fields,
back at his home at last.

Happy Retirement

All Grand National winners do a certain amount of public appearances: Aldaniti was no exception. His season started almost immediately with an invitation to kick-off at a charity football match in aid of the Injured Jockeys' Fund, at Hayes in Middlesex. A team of jump jockeys were playing the Racing All-stars. Aldaniti was led on to the centre of the pitch and the ball was placed on the ground in front of him. He studied it carefully, lifted a front leg, and pushed it forward.

From that start, which was a great success, he was off to Huntingdon to help raise money for the Save the Grand National Campaign—a cause that was of particular interest to his owner. The famous racecourse was in danger of being lost unless money could be found to purchase it. Then there were three days at the Royal Cornwall Show, where the National winner is always one of the attractions.

The only time that Aldaniti came near to disgracing himself was when Josh and Peter Double took him to Lingfield Childrens' Hospital for a special fund raising day where he was to be one of several celebrity guests. There were a lot of people milling round him, keeping Josh and Peter busy, when two of the other guests, Miss U.K. and Roy Castle, came over to meet Aldaniti.

When he saw the beauty queen Aldaniti was obviously enthralled. He pushed out his nose to greet her with such enthusiasm that he very nearly knocked her over. Duly ticked off by Peter, he was kept on a tighter rein. Roy Castle was chatting about the horse to Josh, and when he had heard that Aldaniti was really gentle to ride—a real Christian, as Josh put it—he asked if he could have a go. Unfortunately when Josh legged him up, Roy landed just behind the saddle, on Aldaniti's loins. The next thing he knew was that he was flying through the air to land on his back on the unyielding surface of a hard tennis court. Aldaniti had put in such a big buck that he had also broken the surcingle that held his saddle on. Luckily Roy was not hurt, taking it well while the crowd thought it very amusing.

The next outing was to Windsor Great Park to the Great Picnic held in aid of Cancer Research. Bob had been invited at the specific request of the Queen to be presented to her. It was a massive occasion with hundreds of people, just the kind of situation that Aldaniti by then really enjoyed. Happy to receive his share of attention, he managed to behave himself that day as he normally did.

In between these engagements Aldaniti was spending the days out in the fields at Barkfold Manor with his friends, coming in at night to avoid the danger of injury to himself or any of the others. It was not the usual pattern of the summers at Barkfold that he enjoyed so much. But he was becoming thoroughly professional as a celebrity guest, well aware when he was the centre of attention, appreciating all the fuss that was made of him, so that he did not appear to miss the complete freedom that he would have had in other years.

He was again guest of honour at the small office party that Nick held annually for the staff who worked for him in London. Each summer they were invited to Barkfold Manor for the day, and that year Aldaniti was on parade for them after lunch.

To keep him ready for these appearances he was kept in light work, being ridden out quietly once or twice a week. Alexandra was home from school by then and was helping in the stables as much as she could, often with the preparations necessary before Aldaniti went off to raise money. Before long she was helping to exercise him too, finding him easy to ride round the roads and lanes.

In the meantime Nick and Valda had been planning a party for all their friends to celebrate Aldaniti's win. Towards the end of July the marquee went up on the lawn. All the flowers and decorations inside were to be in royal blue and white —Nick's racing colours. On the morning of the party Aldaniti had been kept in as he was to make a special appearance in the evening. Beryl decided that he would get bored cooped up in the stable all day, so she took him out to see what he would make of the marquee. Aldaniti did not appear to mind the canvas at all, so the pair went inside, where the flower arrangements were being finished. Aldaniti inspected everything, as well as all the people who were busily trying to get it ready.

Later in the evening, plaited, shining and pleased with life, Aldaniti paraded for the guests with his natural ease and presence, looking every inch the National winner that was the reason for the party. Among the guests that night were David Barron and his wife Chris, who had not seen him close to for a long time. As his father's representative that night, David felt very proud of the horse that had started life as the ugliest foal on Harrowgate stud eleven years before.

"He's come a long way," he said somewhat wistfully, as if he would have given a lot to have been the one who had trained him to become the success that he was.

"He certainly has," his wife agreed as she watched the horse that she had named. She was thinking back to when her children were much smaller. "Renardeau had two more by Derek H, didn't she?"

"Yes," David said. "She was a good mare—except where that chap was concerned. Still, it didn't do him any harm."

As Aldaniti was led away, walking out proudly, carrying himself with the confident movement that is often found in the more successful horses, Chris agreed with her husband. The fact that Polly had not had enough milk for Aldaniti had not made the slightest difference to the horse in the end.

When the Chiddingfold, Leconfield and Cowdray Hunt held their open day and terrier show in Petworth Park, Aldaniti was a natural guest. Valda was a member of the hunt, and Nick had been delighted to let the horse go for the day.

Every summer the Embiricoses lent their land for the Pony Club to hold a working rally. In August 1981 about fifty children and their ponies turned up for instruction in the morning. Then, after lunch, while the ponies ate and rested, Aldaniti was brought out for them to see, and Beryl told them about his problems. She explained how good a patient he had been during the long six months when he had chipped his hind-leg and had been confined to his box, and how he had again been calm and quiet when he had broken-down on the off-fore, and of all the long, slow work that had gone into getting him into condition for the National.

Afterwards the children crowded round the big chestnut horse, looking at his legs, stroking him, stuffing him with peppermints. In his element, Aldaniti responded gently to the attention, once again lapping it up.

Later in the month there was one more parade for the villagers of Kirdford. Then Aldaniti had the longest spell in the fields that summer, idling away the time, quickly getting his usual grass tummy, romping with the other horses in the summer evenings, really unwinding at last.

Nick had by then decided that Aldaniti would go into training for the following season with the Grand National as his target once again, partly because he was still a very young horse in himself and Nick did not want him to become bored, but also because other owners enjoy the chance to run their horses against a previous winner. Before that would happen there were still more public appearances in store for Aldaniti.

It is not every day that the shoppers in London's Covent Garden find themselves face to face with a large horse. But they did the day that *Champion's Story* was launched, the book written by Bob and his close friend Jonathan Powell. The organisers had considered Aldaniti a natural member of the party, and had arranged a straw-bedded pen for him to stand in. The horse looked far less alarmed by the hustle and bustle of London than many of the people who saw him standing there, posing for the cameras.

By then Aldaniti knew that when cameras were around everyone loved it if he rose to the occasion, and he always managed to, looking extra alert, every inch the winner, as natural as only the professional model can be. When Jonathan held open a copy of the book in front of him, Aldaniti appeared to be reading about himself with immense interest, while Bob and Peter Double looked on.

Then it was back to the slow build up of work that would prepare him for training at Findon. His legs toughened up, better and straighter than they had been at the same stage the year before. His chances for the coming 1981–1982 season began to look hopeful as his grass fat turned into muscle with the hill work round Bedham and the introduction of cantering in the fields and woods around Barkfold. A sitting—or standing—for his portrait was fitted in, and then one more engagement was arranged before he would be off to Findon.

Early in December the BBC had been in touch with the Embiricoses concerning their annual Sports Personality of the Year Show. Bob Champion was one of the contenders for the award in 1981. The BBC wanted to send an outside broadcast unit to Barkfold Manor on the day of the programme, and had asked if Nick and Valda, Josh and Althea and Beryl and Aldaniti could all be there. The Embiricoses thought that they would merely be televised as back-up for Bob when his turn came to show how he had come to be nominated for the award. As it was to be filmed in the evening, the Embiricoses went to Newmarket the evening before, as they had already arranged to do, for a day's pheasant shooting with friends.

They drove straight back to Barkfold, to find their home coated in snow and, to their amazement, a hundred foot television mast behind the stables plus umpteen large vehicles parked in the yard and drive. Josh and Althea arrived on time, and—well wrapped up against the cold—they all trooped out to the stables. A television monitor had been installed in Aldaniti's box, with cameras and lights and all the other paraphernalia that goes with filming. Beryl was holding the horse who appeared totally unconcerned by the strange equipment all over the stables and in his box—the only member of the party neither stiff with cold nor wooden with stage fright.

The programme in London started, which those at Barkfold could all watch in Aldaniti's box. When their turn came to be interviewed, the television cameras started rolling at Barkfold and Frank Bough, from the studio in London, interviewed each in turn. They didn't find it easy with just a television set to talk to, but they all tried their best to help Bob.

To the total amazement of the Embiricoses and the Giffords, as well as Beryl, they were then told that they had, as a group which included Bob, been chosen for "The Outstanding Team of the Year Award" of the BBC 1981 Sports Personality of the Year Show.

There are a lot of superstitions connected with racing, so with Nick being a superstitious person anyway, it was decided that if Aldaniti was going to run in the National again, everything would have to happen exactly as it had done the year before. December 22nd—a year to the day since he had travelled to Findon in 1980—the horse-box arrived at Barkfold Manor to take Aldaniti back into training. In the Gifford yard the same box was waiting for him, with the same lad to do him. With Josh again riding him in all his work, Aldaniti began to follow, as closely as possible, the same build up to the race.

There were one or two differences though. For a start Bob had married Jo Beswick, and there were still occasional inter-

ruptions to the routine for publicity sessions. Christmas Eve
with the Gifford yard covered in snow, saw Bob appear i
Nick's racing colours to stand outside with Aldaniti and tw
very attractive girls. The horse and his jockey were bein
presented with the Heineken Christmas Award—beer fo
Bob and a medal for Aldaniti.

Then it was back into serious training. Although Nick wa
interested in Aldaniti's progress, he felt none of the sam
excitement and anticipation of the first National. He was eve
away on holiday with Valda when Aldaniti was due to race fo
the first time—in the same Whitbread Trial Handicap 'Chas
that he had won so effortlessly in 1981. In 1982 he did not ru
well, though. Getting off to a late start he stayed at the bac
and came in last.

The race did not damage his legs, so it was decided to ru
him again on March 6th at Haydock. As Bob had been injure
in a fall a few days earlier from one of Nick's novice horses, th
ride was given to Ron Barry. In the Greenall Whitle
Breweries Handicap 'Chase he went better, running prom
isingly to come in sixth. Not the success of 1981, but a goo
enough performance to make Josh think that they stood
chance in the Grand National.

Just a week before the race, Bob came to grief when anothe
of Nick's horses, African Prince, fell, taking the jockey wit
him. Although concussed, Bob could remember how stric
course doctors were, but he had no idea where he was or wh
he had been riding. When he got to the changing room, befor
he went near the doctor, he quickly asked friends to fill in th
missing pieces—what day it was, what fence he had fallen at
where the meeting was and who his horse had been. H
managed to learn the answers by heart and scrape through hi
interview with the doctor.

By the morning of the National he was fine, although he ha
not been so good during the week when Josh had asked hin
down to Findon to ride, partly to see for himself how th
jockey really was. At that Aintree meeting of 1982 Aldanit
was the only ride Bob had. His weight problem had increase

drastically with the chemotherapy treatment, and he was talking of retiring as a jockey after the National. But both Bob and Josh felt that they were in with a good chance. Aldaniti's legs had stood up to training well, he had been able to take more work and was therefore fitter than the year before, and also he knew the course.

The pre-race briefing was virtually the same—to hunt round for the first circuit, wide on the outside. Then, if they were in with a chance, to start making their way to the front. Unless Bob got run away with again, in which case he really would not have much say in the matter.

Eight fell at the first fence—among them Aldaniti. He had overjumped to the extent that there was no way he could save himself, and nothing that Bob could do. It was exactly as if Aldaniti recognised where he was, remembered how he had enjoyed the big fences before, said, "Yippee, here we are again," and threw himself into the fun of the race with such a prodigious leap that even he did not stand a chance of landing on all four feet. Horse and jockey got to their feet with no sign that anything was wrong. Aldaniti, who had never fallen in his life before, saw the other horses disappearing over the next fence and set off after them as if he was determined not to be left out of the race just through one careless mistake. Loose horses are one of the most dangerous hazards in the National, both to the others and to themselves. Riderless, Aldaniti threw himself at the fences, jumping freely and fluently until another loose horse in front of him spotted a way off the course, and Aldaniti followed. Still galloping, they hit the tarmac road used by the camera cars and ambulances, until Aldaniti was eventually caught by the flat trainer Peter Walwyn.

Nick was only briefly depressed at Aldaniti's failure. After the seemingly fateful events of the dream win the year before, neither he nor Valda had felt anything like the same excitement in 1982. To them a National "double" would have been marvellous—but it could never touch or even compare with the win of 1981. That had been unique, one of the most outstanding events of their lives, to remain so always. Aldaniti had not been bought by them to win the National but as a nice young horse that they had watched through a promising career, as well as his dreadful injuries. His success had been an unexpected bonus that they would always be thankful for and in no way take for granted.

Nick retired him from racing immediately, and within a few days Aldaniti was once again home at Barkfold—this time with filling in the suspensory under the knee in his near fore—left front—leg. Beryl put him on to a routine of cold water hosing and iced bandages, to try and reduce the swelling and get rid of the heat. He had to be kept in, but was taken out for a pick of grass each day. Gradually the leg did improve until he was well enough to be turned loose in the all-weather school once again to get rid of his usual high spirits.

Then he was turned out with the other geldings for time and rest to heal the leg completely, and also to enjoy the summer to the full which he had been unable to do the previous year. When he was at last sound, as well as rested, Nick had to decide what to do with Aldaniti. He wanted the horse to go on being used, although he knew that any form of racing was out of the question or Aldaniti would break down completely and could well then have to be destroyed.

His first idea was to offer Aldaniti to Bob as a hack. Bob had started training and would need a horse to ride out on. Unfortunately Jo Champion had just been offered another very well known retired racehorse named Pendil for that purpose, which she had accepted. So the Champions did not have room for another non-competitive mouth to feed. Bob came up with the solution for Aldaniti. He had just started the Bob Champion Cancer Trust, a registered charity with the specific purpose of supporting research into cancer in young people. His idea was that Aldaniti should go on working for charity, and that any money he made would go into the Bob Champion Trust, specifically for Cancer Research at the Royal Marsden Hospital, Sutton, Surrey, where he had been cured. Once the arrangements were worked out, it looked as if Aldaniti would be leading a busy and useful life after all, within the limitations that his various injuries would allow, which was exactly what his owner wanted.

About the same time that Aldaniti's retirement was being planned so carefully, a major feature film was also under discussion—to be called *Champions*, based on Bob's book, *Champion's Story*. The producer, Peter Shaw, and the script-writer, Evan Jones, asked the Embiricoses if they could come down to Barkfold Manor to meet both them and Aldaniti. They would need a horse to play Aldaniti in the film. As soon as he had read the original book Peter Shaw had wondered whether it would be possible to use Aldaniti, partly because he preferred to stick as near to the truth as possible and partly because he expected that, being the success he was, Aldaniti would have that little bit of extra presence that would make him stand out.

As soon as Peter Shaw and Evan Jones saw Aldaniti, they were convinced that they had been right to want to use him. When Beryl was asked if she thought he would mind the lights and cameras and crowds that would be involved, she was well able to assure them that he would not. After all it was hardly a year since he had had the lot in his box—and he had shown no objection at all. Quite the opposite, in fact—hamming it up and playing to the camera, completely at ease. It was agreed that he would be ready for filming in April 1983, with the proviso that he did not do any galloping or jumping in the film.

While Beryl began to get Aldaniti up into work again and starting on the vital walking needed to get him fit enough for the filming, a search began for his "double". No two chestnut horses are exactly the same colour. Aldaniti's unusual white blaze, right down the front of his head, was going to cause problems for the make-up department as well. The double would also have to be capable of jumping the National fences at Aintree, and be suitable for the star of the film, John Hurt, who was playing Bob Champion, to ride.

To satisfy all these requirements, Aldaniti ended up having six doubles—more than Roger Moore or Elizabeth Taylor!

The main one, though, was Flitgrove, owned by Lord Vestey, who had run in the National in 1979 but had unfortunately pulled up at the twenty-seventh fence. Under the supervision of Terry Biddlecombe, John Hurt was to ride Flitgrove in quite a lot of the scenes as he had a lovely mouth and was very quiet. Another double was spotted racing at Cheltenham, Hartley Hill. The nearest in looks to Aldaniti, he was to be used for most of the jumping sequences, when the jockey John Burke would be standing in for John Hurt. Hartley Hill had an intense dislike of any fence with an open ditch in front of it though, so the next horse to be taken on was a point-to-pointer, Gingerbread House, who belonged to Sally Webber, who said that as long as he just did the open ditches and no more it would be all right. Various other horses were found as well for different reasons, one of the main ones being that Aldaniti was so strong as soon as he felt grass underneath him that very few people could ride him.

As the original Aldaniti gradually got fitter it was decided to take him back to Guy Harwood's all-weather gallop for a work out. Beryl rode him at a canter, feeling the full power of the motor behind her. His leg survived the faster work, which had been part of the exercise and looked good for the filming and future work after that.

Filming with animals is meant to be as difficult as with children. Director John Irving had that problem to cope with as well as the fact that at that time no one had successfully filmed racing sequences and captured the true feel of the sport to satisfy the critical cinema goers. Both Bob Champion and Terry Biddlecombe (an ex-jockey himself)—acting as racing adviser to John Hurt—had both dared the director not to make the usual mess of the racing scenes, a challenge he met with careful planning and dedication.

When Aldaniti found himself on Lambourn training gallops with the other horses that would be in the film with him, he began to think that he was back in training again. Beryl had gone with him, first of all to look after the horse and ride him out when he was not being used for filming. She found that out on the gallops, Aldaniti had an extra spring in his step again, an extra edge that she had not noticed before, as if he genuinely thought that he had returned to the life he loved.

One of the first scenes that Aldaniti was asked to do was for the opening sequence of the film, a horse galloping alone on the downs. After the first take Beryl was asked if they could try it again. Although she had strict instructions from Nick that Aldaniti was to do no more than canter, she agreed, adding the condition that he must not go too fast. He was being ridden by the jockey John Burke. The second time they filmed the scene Aldaniti began to take a hold—wanting to go. Again it was not quite right. Beryl agreed that Aldaniti could do it again, but that would be the last time as he had done enough that day. Aldaniti thought differently. Knowing exactly where to go he really got into his stride—so much so that the jockey could hardly stop him.

The next day Aldaniti was off to Ascot to parade on behalf of the Save the Grand National Campaign. It was May, and a race meeting. Plaited up and walking round the parade ring with Rubstic and Red Rum, Aldaniti really came alive as if he thought that after working on the Lambourn Downs with the racehorses in the film, he must be going racing again himself. When Beryl took him back to his box and undid his plaits and he realised that he was not going to race, Aldaniti became so unhappy that he stood with his head in the corner and refused to talk to anyone. Even Alexandra was ignored for the first time by the friendly horse when she went out to see him.

Beryl left him alone for a while and watched the next race. When she got back to Aldaniti he was still too unhappy to notice her, and did not pick up until he was back on the film set again with horses all round him.

As Aldaniti was so strong to ride, especially with grass underneath him, John Hurt did most of his scenes on the double Flitgrove. The business of matching his colour exactly to Aldaniti's and making-up the white blaze and sock was quite a problem. Hair sprays were used on Flitgrove's body. Grease-paint for the white markings. Beryl was the one who knew exactly what Aldaniti looked like and she found herself involved with re-creating his likeness with the doubles.

However well made-up the doubles were, it was not long before the film crew could tell when they were filming Aldaniti himself. His natural presence made him stand out in a way that outshone the rest of the horses and was instantly noticeable. He played to the cameras as if he knew exactly what he was meant to be doing, not in the least perturbed by the lights and noises—unlike some of his doubles.

One scene that proved a problem was when a string of racehorses, with "Aldaniti" in front, had to gallop straight for the camera which was low on the ground, swerving away at the last minute. This was too much for the double being used for the scene. He was shying away from the camera long before he reached it. After several takes, none of them any use, there was only one answer—Aldaniti himself would have to do it, although he had officially done his stint for that day and had been put back in his box.

Beryl agreed that he could come out again, and fetched him. With the camera in position, the horses were lined up ready to try again. When "Action" was called, they began to canter. Aldaniti saw the camera, looked straight into it, kept moving towards it, obeyed the command to turn away at the very last minute—still watching the lens. The take was perfect—exactly what had been wanted. Done in one go once Aldaniti was used.

To achieve a realistic Grand National in the film involved working to a tight schedule. Normally the tents and signs are pulled down the Sunday after the race at Aintree. That year though, the racecourse organisers had agreed to leave them up, as well as to repair the fences, for the film to be made. The film company moved up to Liverpool immediately after the National meeting was over, and used as many as 12,000 extras a day for the crowd scenes.

The film race itself had been planned well in advance on a story-board, where each scene is drawn so that the director and producer know exactly what they want to happen at each take. Filmed fence by fence, with a mixture of racehorses and point-to-pointers playing the parts of the horses who actually competed in 1981, it resulted in one of the most breathtaking racing sequences ever to be seen on the cinema screen—and, amazingly, not one of the horses was hurt in the making of it.

By the end of the filming Aldaniti was in nearly every scene, except for the ones where he had to be galloping or jumping. The magical opening shot, of the chestnut horse galloping in slow motion across the downs in the early morning, is Aldaniti, and again it is him each time the "dream" sequence is shown throughout the film. It is the real Aldaniti hobbling off the course at Sandown, the lameness caused by a hobble which gave him no pain at all, recapturing exactly that tragic day when it looked as if his career was over and Bob's future recovery thrown into doubt.

When his days as a film star were over it was back to Barkfold and the quiet life again for Aldaniti—and his friend New Arctic, a horse that had done a bit of everything during his life and been lent to Valda as a hunter by a friend, George Sloane. In his previous summers at Barkfold, New Arctic had always been a bit of a loner, not making friends with the other horses, not looking particularly good when he came into work again—at least, not as good as he should have done after a summer at grass. As Aldaniti was going to be coming and going all the time during the filming in 1983 and with charity appearances, Beryl had decided that he would be better, when he was at home, to be turned out with just one other gelding. She had chosen New Arctic as the other horse. The two had, surprisingly, become friends, but not so closely attached that they could not be separated. When Aldaniti was taken away from the field the pair would call to each other, but New Arctic would then settle down quietly on his own. Each time that Aldaniti returned to the field they would greet each other vocally and canter off together for a bit of fun before settling down to eat. By the end of the summer New Arctic came in looking better than he had done before.

Having a friend whom he actually got on with had helped him to relax and do himself well for a change.

Aldaniti's comings and goings continued throughout the summer and he made charity appearances all over the place. One of the engagements he enjoyed most was competing against the minute ponies in the Shetland Grand National. As the fences were only one-foot-six inches high, and the speed not exactly demanding, he was allowed to compete. It was at Newmarket, on Town Plate day in October 1983, with Bob in the saddle. They were coming up to the last with Aldaniti lying second to a diminutive Shetland. The little girl riding it turned and looked up at Bob—the expression on her face saying, "Please don't let him beat me." Bob could not resist the plea. It was not so easy convincing Aldaniti. Bob had to take a really tight pull to make him come in second, beaten by a short head, by a pony that hardly came up to the big chestnut's knees. The winner's grin of satisfaction made it well worth while, even if Aldaniti did not appreciate it.

The winter of 1983 saw Aldaniti clipped out and living in, with an American film company coming over to England to make a short film about him and Bob Champion that is intended to be released on television throughout the world. He had to be kept fit and in work with that coming along so when the Lawn meet of the Chiddingfold, Leconfield and Cowdray Hunt was held at Barkfold Manor, it was decided that Aldaniti should put in an appearance. The day before Wilf Millam took him for a canter in the fields as it was some time since he had ridden Aldaniti, and he wanted to get the feel of him again.

By the end of the session Wilf's arms were numb. Aldaniti had pulled like a train. At the meet he was on his best behaviour, standing in front of Barkfold Manor with hounds milling around him and underneath him, never putting a hoof wrong. As the ground was very soft, Nick had said that Wilf could take him out when the hunt moved off, and follow for an hour or two. To his surprise, as he had expected Aldaniti to pull even harder when he was cantering in a crowd, the big horse responded to Wilf's voice, did not pull, and put the regular hunters to shame when it came to jumping a flooded stream.

Obviously his retirement will continue with enough interesting work to keep Aldaniti both occupied and happy. Fourteen years old now, he could well go on for many years. Nothing that might damage his legs again will be asked of him, though. Everyone who rides or owns horses has one that stands out in their life. For Nick Embiricos that one is Aldaniti, who means far too much to his owner for him to allow any unnecessary risks to be taken with him.

In the meantime, eating his head off at Barkfold, is a four year old gelding, Royal Gambit, by the same sire as Aldaniti and as yet unraced. So far there are no signs of similarity between Royal Gambit and his half-brother. Where Aldaniti was a pleasure to break in, Royal Gambit made the job a nightmare, for a while getting rid of everyone who tried to ride him. When he goes into training in the autumn of this year it could be anyone's guess how he will do. He is a totally unknown quantity, as was Aldaniti when Nick bought him, and that is how he likes his horses. Watching Royal Gambit develop, the ups and downs, the good and the bad, will provide Nick with the excitement and pleasure he gets from National Hunt racing. Whichever way the youngster goes, Aldaniti's success was an added bonus—a once in a lifetime dream—that will never be forgotten, or taken for granted.

Aldaniti's Racing Career

25th June 1970:
Foaled at Harrowgate Stud, Darlington, by Derek H out of Renardeau.

September 1973:
Broken by David Barron at Northallerton.

May 1974:
Sold at Ascot Bloodstock sales to Josh Gifford.

1974–1975 season

10th January, 1975:
ASCOT. Silver Doctor Novices' Hurdle (Div 2) for 5-year-olds, run over 2 miles.
Jockey: R. Champion. Weight 11st. Starting price 33–1. Placed 1st, beating Sunyboy by 4 lengths. 17 ran.
Owner/Trainer: Josh Gifford.

8th February:

WOLVERHAMPTON. Panama Cigar Hurdle (qualifier) for 5yo, run over 2 miles.

Jockey: R. Champion. Weight 11st 7lbs. Starting price 11–8 (fav). Placed 4th, 9½ lengths behind the winner Super Trojan. 18 ran.

Owner: S.N. Embiricos. Trainer: Josh Gifford.

26th February:

LINGFIELD. Orpington Novices' Hurdle (Div 2) for 5 and 6 yo, run over 2 miles.

Jockey: R. Champion. Weight 11st. Starting price 4–1. Placed 2nd, beaten by 1 length by Rossini. 13 ran.

Owner: S.N. Embiricos. Trainer: Josh Gifford.

13th March:

CHELTENHAM. Sun Alliance Novices' Hurdle, run over 2 miles 4 furlongs.

Jockey: R. Champion. Weight 11st. 7lbs. Starting price 20–1. Placed 4th, 18 lengths behind the winner Davy Lad. 20 ran.

Owner: S.N. Embiricos. Trainer: Josh Gifford.

10th April:

ASCOT. Sardan Novices' Hurdle, run over 2 miles 4 furlongs.

Jockey: R. Champion. Weight 11st. 7lbs. Starting price 12–1. Placed 3rd, 11 lengths behind the winner Sunyboy.

Owner: S.N. Embiricos. Trainer: Josh Gifford.

1975–1976 season

1st January 1976:

WINDSOR. Touchen End Handicap Hurdle for 6 yo, run over 2 miles 6 furlongs.

Jockey: R. Champion. Weight 11st 2lbs. Starting price 11–2.

Placed 3rd, 14 lengths behind the winner, Drum Major. 16 ran.
Owner: S.N. Embiricos. Trainer: Josh Gifford.

10th January:
SANDOWN. William Hill Handicap Hurdle, run over 2 miles 5 furlongs 75 yds.
Jockey: R. Champion. Weight 10st 8lbs. Starting price 7–1. Placed 7th. 14 ran.
Owner: S.N. Embiricos. Trainer: Josh Gifford.

Found to be lame. Fired.

1976–1977 season

16th February 1977:
ASCOT. Sapling Novices' Chase, run over 2 miles.
Jockey: R. Champion. Weight 11st 3lbs. Starting price 20–1. Placed 2nd, beaten by 8 lengths by Tree Tangle. 8 ran.
Owner: S.N. Embiricos. Trainer Josh Gifford.

4th March:
NEWBURY. Burford Novices' Chase (Div 2), run over 3 miles.
Jockey: R. Champion. Weight 11st 11lbs. Starting price 13–8 (fav). Blundered at 5th and unseated jockey. 12 ran.
Owner: S.N. Embiricos. Trainer: Josh Gifford.

15th March:
CHELTENHAM. Sun Alliance Chase, run over 3 miles.
Jockey: R. Champion. Weight 11st 4lbs. Starting price 20. Placed 7th. 15 ran.
Owner: S.N. Embiricos. Trainer: Josh Gifford.

1st April:

ASCOT. Heatherwood Novices' Chase, run over 2 miles 4 furlongs.

Jockey: R.Champion. Weight 11st 4lbs. Starting price 6–5 (fav). Placed 1st, beating The Bay Turk by 15 lengths. 12 ran.

Owner: S.N.Embiricos. Trainer: Josh Gifford.

5th April:

FONTWELL. Flansham Novices' Chase (Div 2), run over 2 miles 4 furlongs.

Jockey: R.Champion. Weight 11st 5lbs. Starting price 5–4 (fav). Placed 2nd, beaten by Royal Epic by 3 lengths. 10 ran.

Owner: S.N.Embiricos. Trainer: Josh Gifford.

23 April:

UTTOXETER. Philip Cornes Hunters' Improvement Society Handicap Chase, run over 2 miles 4 furlongs.

Jockey: R.Champion. Weight 11st 9lbs. Starting price 5–4 (fav). Placed 1st, beating Mexican Frolic by 5 lengths. 9 ran.

Owner: S.N.Embiricos. Trainer: Josh Gifford.

1977–1978 season

14th November 1977:

LEICESTER. Leicestershire Silver Fox Handicap Chase, run over 2 miles 4 furlongs.

Jockey: R.Champion. Weight 10st 8lbs. Starting price 3–1. Placed 1st, beating Ireland's Owen by 4 lengths. 6 ran.

Owner: S.N.Embiricos. Trainer: Josh Gifford.

26th November:
NEWBURY. Hennessy Cognac Gold Cup Handicap Chase.
 Run over 3 miles 2 furlongs 82 yds.
Jockey: R.Champion. Weight 10st 7lbs. Starting price 13–1.
 Placed 3rd, five lengths behind the winner Bachelor's
 Hall.
Owner: S.N.Embiricos. Trainer: Josh Gifford.

Found to be lame. Had chipped two pieces of bone off off-hind
leg near fetlock joint. Spent 7 months in the stable.

1978–1979 season

26th December, 1978:
KEMPTON. King George VI Chase, run over 3 miles.
Jockey: R.Champion. Weight 11st. Starting price 25–1.
 Placed 6th 38 lengths behind the winner Gay Spartan.
Owner: S.N.Embiricos. Trainer: Josh Gifford.

11th January 1979:
WINCANTON. John Bull Chase, run over 2 miles 5 fur-
 longs.
Jockey: R.Champion. Weight 11st 6lbs. Starting price 4–1.
 Placed 5th, 28½ lengths behind the winner, Royal Mail. 9
 ran.
Owner: S.N.Embiricos. Trainer: Josh Gifford.

5th March:
WINDSOR. March Handicap Chase, run over 3 miles 4
 furlongs.
Jockey: R.Champion. Weight 11st 5lbs. Starting price 4–1.
 Placed 5th, 7 lengths behind the winner. 10 ran.
Owner: S.N.Embiricos. Trainer: Josh Gifford.

15th March:
CHELTENHAM. Piper Champagne Gold Cup, run over
3¼ miles.
Jockey: R.Champion. Weight 12st. Starting price 40–1.
Placed 3rd, 45 lengths behind the winner Alverton. 14 ran.
Owner: S.N.Embiricos. Trainer: Josh Gifford.

27th March:
SANDOWN. Alanbrooke Memorial Handicap Chase, run
over 3 miles 118 yds.
Jockey: R.Champion. Weight 11st 10lbs. Starting price 11–2.
Placed 1st, beating Strombolus by 2½ lengths. 8 ran.
Owner: S.N.Embiricos. Trainer: Josh Gifford.

21st April:
AYR. William Hill Scottish National Handicap Chase, run
over 4 miles 120 yds.
Jockey: R.Champion. Weight 10st 13lbs. Starting price 9–2
(fav). Placed 2nd, beaten by Fighting Fit by 2½ lengths. 19
ran.
Owner: S.N.Embiricos. Trainer: Josh Gifford.

5th May:
HAYDOCK. Stoke Handicap Chase, run over 3 miles.
Jockey: R.Champion. Weight 12st. Starting price, evens
(fav). Placed 1st, beating Casamayor by 7 lengths. 4 ran.
Owner: S.N.Embiricos. Trainer: Josh Gifford.

1979–1980 season

30th November 1979:
SANDOWN. Ewell Handicap Chase, run over 3 miles, 5
furlongs, 18 yds.
Jockey: R.Rowe. Weight 11st 3lbs. Starting price 13–8 (fav).
Pulled up lame two out from home.
Owner: S.N.Embiricos. Trainer: Josh Gifford.

Broken down on off-fore.

Aldaniti's Racing Career

1980–1981 season

11th February 1981:
ASCOT. Whitbread Trial Handicap Chase, run over 3
   miles.
Jockey: R.Champion. Weight 11st 7lbs. Starting price 14–1.
   Placed 1st, beating Royal Charley by 4 lengths. 8 ran.
Owner: S.N.Embiricos. Trainer: Josh Gifford.

4th April:
AINTREE. Sun Grand National Handicap Chase, run over
   4 miles 4 furlongs.
Jockey: R.Champion. Weight 10st 13lbs. Starting price 10–1.
   Placed 1st, beating the favourite Spartan Missile by 4
   lengths. 39 ran.
Owner: S.N.Embiricos. Trainer: Josh Gifford.

1981–1982 season

10th February 1982:
ASCOT. Whitbread Trial Handicap Chase, run over 3
   miles.
Jockey: R.Rowe. Weight 10st 9lbs. Starting price evens.
   Placed 8th. 9 ran.
Owner: S.N.Embiricos. Trainer: Josh Gifford.

6th March:
HAYDOCK. Grenall Whitley Breweries Handicap Chase,
   run over 3 miles.
Jockey: R.Barry. Weight 10st 9lbs. Starting price 20–1.
   Placed 6th. 8 ran.
Owner: S.N.Embiricos. Trainer: Josh Gifford.

3rd April:

AINTREE. Sun Grand National Handicap Chase. Run over
4 miles 4 furlongs.

Jockey: R.Champion. Weight 11st 9lbs. Starting price 12–1.
Fell at 1st fence.

Owner: S.N.Embiricos. Trainer: Josh Gifford.

Immediately retired from racing